HETAL ADESARA was born and brought up in Jamshedpur and moved to Mumbai when she was 18. She graduated from Sophia College, Mumbai, and went on to get a diploma in Journalism from Xavier Institute of Communications.

In her 10-year career, Hetal started off as a journalist at Indiantelevision.com. Thereafter, she headed the editorial team Businessofcinema.com, which she also co-founded.

During her stint with the film industry, she worked on the landmark Hindi film *3 Idiots* as assistant to producer Vidhu Vinod Chopra. In 2012, she assisted director Rohan Sippy on *Nautanki Saala,* starring Ayushmann Khurrana, where she also donned the hat of script-supervisor. Most recently, Hetal has worked on the IIFA Awards, Macau (2013) and IIFA Awards, Tampa Bay (2014) as Executive Producer for television and digital content.

Being an avid movie watcher, Hetal was always drawn to the fantastical world of films. It was her passion for writing and creating a whole new world with words that made her take a giant leap of faith when she quit her job to write her first book.

Matrimonial Mocktales is Hetal's debut novel. Her personal blog can be found at www.adesarahetal.blogspot.in. She tweets with the handle @HetalAdesara

Matrimonial Mocktales

Hetal Adesara

OM
Om Books International

First published in 2014 by

OM

Om Books International

Corporate & Editorial Office
A-12, Sector 64, Noida 201 301
Uttar Pradesh, India
Phone: +91 120 477 4100
Email: editorial@ombooks.com
Website: www.ombooksinternational.com

Sales Office
4379/4B, Prakash House, Ansari Road
Darya Ganj, New Delhi 110 002, India
Phone: +91 11 2326 3363, 2326 5303
Fax: +91 11 2327 8091
Email: sales@ombooks.com
Website: www.ombooks.com

ISBN: 978-93-84225-70-4

10 9 8 7 6 5 4 3 2 1

Printed in India

For my best friend forever

ANEESHA GREWAL

My angel, my mother, my sister, my soulmate. You were all this and more. I miss you every day but I'll wait to join you in another world, where our reunion would mean bringing the roof down in the only way we've ever known!

And my grandmother

JASWANTI ADESARA

Prologue

Truth is stranger than fiction, but it is because fiction is obliged to stick to possibilities; truth isn't.

—Mark Twain

All Rhea had ever wanted was the perfect Mills & Boon romance and everything that came with it. But given the world that she lived in, it was too much to ask. Or was it?

She had been raised in a traditional Sikh family in Jalandhar where it was unfathomable for a girl to be unmarried at age 25, let alone 33. But here she was, a single, independent girl in search of Mr. Right. Hers seemed to be a common everyday saga: a girl with dreams looking for love, romance and the elusive happily-ever-after. She believed.

Rhea's search had begun at a very early age, but not of her own accord. At 15, she was engaged to a 23-year-old boy! But that story didn't go as her parents had planned and hence the better part of her early young life more or less revolved around finding 'a suitable boy'.

In this pursuit, there were many Mr. Wrongs. Her first step into the arena of love began on the wrong foot; little did she know, the initial jinx would haunt her for a long, long time.

1

Short, Fair, Handsome

1995
Jalandhar

'Rhea, be ready by 5.30 tomorrow morning. We're going to Delhi.'

'We? Me too? Why? But I have school tomorrow.' Rhea looked skeptically at her father, Jaspal, and her mother, Gurleen, who made the announcement nonchalantly, while watching a Hindi soap, *Tara*, on Zee TV.

'Yes, you too. We're going to see a boy for you,' said her mother matter-of-factly.

'Whatttttt?' exclaimed Rhea with an incredulous smirk, half hoping it was some kind of practical joke. But when she realised her usually strict mother was serious, the mirth fled her face as quickly as it had appeared. Wide-eyed, she looked at her father, hoping to find answers or even an escape route. Instead, she saw his tight-lipped smile. Jaspal was a rich, educated and progressive farmer in Jalandhar, who had single-handedly climbed up the business ranks. From owning two small pieces of land, he was now the owner of the biggest tractor-manufacturing factory in the city. He was relatively easygoing but his wife, Gurleen, with her old-school views and her fervent belief that a girl's ultimate place was in her husband's house, was the exact opposite. While Jaspal's peers hung on to his every word, Gurleen was clearly the commanding officer at home.

'But, Mumma, I'm only 15! I don't want to get married so soon. I even have my Board Exams in a few months,' said Rhea, hoping her last declaration would save her.

But she knew there was no getting away.

'We have your best interests at heart. This may seem early to you but we're not getting you married immediately. Obviously, there will be a period of courtship. He's a nice boy from a good and well-to-do family. What's also important is that we know them well. He's Charan Uncle's sister's son. You might even remember meeting him at Charan Uncle and Jaswinder Auntie's 15th wedding anniversary!' said Gurleen.

'What's his name?' asked Rhea.

'Happy Singh.'

'Mummaaaa! What's his real name?'

'*Beta,* his real name is Happy.'

Rhea couldn't help laughing, much to her mother's annoyance. But one stern look from her put an end to that.

This couldn't be happening to her, she thought. First, she might have to face the embarrassment of telling her friends that she could be getting hitched at such a young age. To top it all, the boy's name was Happy Singh! *Happy??!!!* Rhea could feel her brain going into overdrive.

Of course, she had come across boys with nicknames like Happy, Rinku, Tinku, Toni, Gullu *et al* but couldn't think of anyone who had these monikers as actual first names. The girls at school would surely mock her. She couldn't help but dread the reactions she would get from Aditi and the boys.

After overcoming her initial hysteria, Rhea tried to picture Happy Singh with the information she had at hand. Her first concern was whether he fulfilled her clichéd but ever so critical 'Tall–Dark–Handsome' criteria.

She vaguely remembered that Charan Uncle's son, Randeep, had pointed Happy out to her at the anniversary party from a distance, referring to him as his cousin from Delhi. At best, he could be described as 'Short–Fair–Handsome' and as for his name, she was trying hard not to think about it!

'At least he's handsome. And being fair is not bad either,' Rhea told herself, her mind finding solace in the fact. But she needed to find out more about him; his age, his interests, his educational qualifications, his zodiac sign and so many other things—her mind was preparing a questionnaire. She started with enquiring about his age. Gurleen told her that he was 'only' 23, which made him eight years older than her! Before she had time to absorb this bit of information, her mother was rattling off important instructions.

'Bittu Maharaj has said green clothes will be lucky for you. Wear your green *salwar kameez* on the train and pack the heavy red one that we bought a couple of months back. Also pack a few jeans and tops. And wear your silver flat *chappals,* not heels.'

On hearing that last directive, all 5 feet 6 inches of her were on alert. 'Flat footwear? Why, Mumma? Is he shorter than me? I hope he's not shorter than me! I don't want to marry a guy who's shorter than me!' she said anxiously, despite having accepted the fact that there was no running away from this inevitable 'first meeting'.

'Don't be silly, Rhea. We won't make you meet someone who is shorter than you. He's almost the same height as you and that's why your mother is asking you not to wear heels. And we're just going to see him. Marriage will come much later,' Jaspal tried to explain, speaking for the first time since the conversation had started.

Hearing this made her feel a tad better but she was still crestfallen about the shoes. As if it wasn't enough that his name was Happy, he might be the reason she would have to forego wearing high heels! In all her 15 years of existence, Rhea had come to realise a deep love for fancy shoes. She could not fathom a life without shoes of the stilettoed variety! The thought of erasing them from her life was appalling. She looked heavenwards and sent out an SOS, 'God, please let him be worthy of my sacrifice.'

During the preparation frenzy for the 'first meeting', Rhea's outlook towards this development had changed from meek resistance to meek acceptance.

'Papa, have you or Mumma told the two brats about this? What should I say to them?' Rhea asked Jaspal after Gurleen had retired for the night. Preet and Geet were Rhea's twin sisters, three years younger than her.

'Don't worry about them. They're too young to understand anything right now. We've told them that we're going to Delhi for two days to attend a function.'

Having packed up the little finery she owned at her age, Rhea and her parents set out the next morning for the rendezvous. To her dismay, the journey was filled with so many dos and don'ts and words of advice from Gurleen that she felt dumb and inept. The volcano of her anger was at eruption point when Gurleen told her to refrain from telling 'them' that she wore lenses. 'It is a big minus,' she said. Ready to spew venom at this latest instruction, Rhea held herself back, but only because Jaspal grabbed her arm in a plea. Not wanting to heat up the environment with her fiery tongue, she rolled her eyes and sealed her lips, resigning to fate.

She turned her attention to the early morning sights visible from the train window, gazing at little children looking at the passing train, women filling water from tube wells, girls washing clothes, men going about their morning jobs and cattle grazing near the railway tracks. None of them knew of the predicament of the young girl, who was a bag of nerves, trepidation coursing through her blood.

The train journey from Jalandhar to Delhi finally came to a chugging halt and Rhea's heart rate accelerated to 160km/hour, putting even the Shatabdi Express to shame.

1995
New Delhi

Two unknown smiling faces welcomed Rhea and her parents at Delhi's Hazrat Nizamuddin railway station. Enquiring how the journey was, they mounted their meagre luggage on the feeble porter's head.

In the midst of polite hellos and saccharine sweet smiles, Gurleen suddenly noticed Rhea's footwear and glared at her. Her eyes seemed to be screaming, 'I told you to wear flats and yet you wore platform heels.' Looking away quickly, Rhea temporarily evaded the fury but she knew it wouldn't be long before she was reprimanded for her defiance.

En route to the meeting with Happy, Rhea's thoughts were anything but. Despite this being her first visit to the Capital, she hardly noticed anything about the vast city because of her mounting nerves while the car sped towards 'destination groom'. In school, she had studied the glorious historical structures in and around Delhi and wondered if the city would be a part of her history too.

Her heartbeat accelerated even more when they reached his house. Dressed in her green *salwar kameez* courtesy the wisdom of Bittu Maharaj, she was a bundle of nerves, twisting and re-twisting her fingers till they hurt.

The sight that awaited Rhea terrified her, making her feel like she was being stared at by a zillion pairs of eyes. *Satnam Wahe Guru! What am I going to do? I want to disappear! Is my hair okay? Is my dress crushed? Is it the right colour?* Her thoughts were running amok. She tried to distract her mind by looking around.

The house was tastefully done up and not as garish as the images Rhea's overactive imagination had thrown up.

After exchanging pleasantries and a round of introductions, Rhea and her parents finally settled down in the drawing room amidst an awkward silence, occasionally interspersed with polite conversation.

Her curiosity got the better of her and she discreetly began scanning the room for the now unavoidable Happy.

'Happy is on his way home from work right now. He should be here any minute,' said one lady, interrupting Rhea's search. She wanted to laugh at the mere mention of his name. How would she keep a straight face when she actually met him?

If only they could hear my thoughts, they would reject this proposal right away, thought Rhea.

That the leader of the 'Mischief Gang' in school was sitting meekly, waiting to be questioned for matrimonial purposes, would be unfathomable to her friends and even her teachers. But Rhea blocked that world from her mind as she tried to concentrate on what was being said, giving polite answers whenever required.

After what seemed like hours, but in reality only 15 minutes, the doorbell rang and Rhea's heartbeat went for a wild and violent gallop.

He's here! Oh, God, please be with me. Let me get through this so we can go back home soon.

The 'Short-Fair-Handsome' Happy Singh walked in and she gave him a tentative smile when they were introduced. Rhea's first thought was that he looked much better than she remembered.

After saying his *Sat Sri Akal*s, he sat down and, almost simultaneously, everyone else started talking. Rhea tried to compose herself and concentrated on bringing her heartbeat down. *You can do it. It's no big deal. There's nothing to be scared about.* She cooed to herself and found some comfort, gradually calming down. But that lasted only for a moment.

'Happy, would you like to show Rhea your room?' his mother, Mona, piped up, sending Rhea's mind into a tizzy. Her eyes grew wide and she frantically looked at Gurleen for some support. Happy sprang to his feet, looking expectantly at Rhea even before Gurleen could give her any reassurance. Not left with much of a choice, Rhea slowly got up. Every hair on the nape of her neck was screaming and confirming what she already knew—all eyes in the room were on her.

Leaving the curious voices behind, she entered his room and took a quick look around. The first thing that struck her was how impersonal it was. Apart from an old picture frame next to his bedside, the room revealed nothing about its occupant.

Rhea scanned the room in search of a chair but found none. She smiled hesitantly at him. 'Nice room,' she said, suddenly finding the quiet atmosphere even more uncomfortable than the gaggle of voices outside the room, and perched herself on the edge of the bed.

After uttering these words, her voice threatened to abandon her. She fiddled with her nails and looked around the uninteresting room hoping to find a conversation starter, which would break the ice.

'Whose picture is that?' she asked, pointing to a table.

'Oh, that's me with my parents when I was young. This was taken at Niagara Falls when we went to Canada,' he replied and went to pick up the frame from the bedside.

She heaved a sigh of relief. Thank God he wasn't one of those people who pronounced the country as 'Kannedaa'. He sat down next to her. Rhea, meanwhile, was telling herself that it shouldn't be so difficult to talk to a stranger.

'That's Mom and Dad and that's me between them,' he said, pointing to himself.

'It's a sweet picture,' Rhea said. Despite her relief at them finally talking to each other, her mind couldn't help but fixate on what he was called. How did he end up with a first name like Happy? She wanted to ask but held her tongue, afraid it might be an obnoxious question.

'A penny for your thoughts,' said Happy, bringing her back from her imaginary world. She was again tempted to ask about his name but instead blurted out, 'Are you a virgin?'

His jaw dropped to the floor on hearing that and Rhea froze. Oh My God! Had she actually just asked him that? She looked as aghast as he did and they both burst out laughing. While Rhea almost died of embarrassment, this query of hers proved to be the real icebreaker.

'I am so sorry! I don't know how that question popped out! I am really sorry. My mother will kill me if she ever finds out.'

Happy was now watching her with a smile and she gave a shy one in return. He was getting a kick out of her embarrassment; she could see it in his eyes.

'That is the most direct question anyone has ever asked me in my entire life,' he said. She was grateful that he had taken her faux pas in his stride. 'Please forget I ever said anything even close to that.' She smiled sheepishly.

'Don't worry about it,' he said.

From that point on, it was easy for Rhea to carry the conversation forward. She decided to take the initiative and asked, 'So this arranged marriage thing…am I the first girl you're meeting or have you met others too? This is a first for me. I'm only 15 years old and, frankly, I had never imagined that I would be meeting a guy for marriage so early on in life.'

'I know what you mean. You are the first girl I'm meeting and I was a bit surprised when I got to know your age and that you were ready to come and see me,' he replied.

'Actually, I didn't really agree but I didn't resist too much either. My mother didn't really give me a choice and I thought there was nothing to lose if I just agreed to come and see you,' said Rhea, casually.

What she didn't tell him was that she planned to decline the proposal if he said 'Yes'. After thinking long and hard since the news was broken to her, she had come to the conclusion that there was no point in resisting her parents and making them angry. After meeting Happy, if she said that she didn't like him, her parents could not force her to agree to the match. That had been her plan when she agreed to the meeting.

'Yes, there's no pressure on you at all,' he said, interrupting her thoughts. Rhea smiled.

'So what are your hobbies?' he asked. In comparison to her earlier Freudian slip, Happy's question seemed almost boringly stereotypical.

For God's sake, say something intelligent, Rhea. Not that you need to or even want to impress him but don't sound like a slob, she told herself.

'Well, I love to read, write and paint,' she found herself saying and then almost did a double take. Rhea could not believe how boringly stereotypical *that* sounded. But it was true.

'Oh, I also love collecting stamps and different kinds of pens,' she added quickly, thinking maybe it sounded a wee bit more exotic than the 'read-write-paint' rubbish. And before she could help it, she heard herself crooning, 'I love collecting stuffed toys too!'

Now there was absolute pandemonium in her mind. *Did you just say stuffed toys? Are you kidding?* There was no looking back now. Maybe this would push him to say 'No' to the proposal. But that consolation didn't take away from the fact that she had made a complete and utter fool of herself by blabbering about stupid childish hobbies.

'That's nice,' she heard Happy say. Rhea smiled, confusion running a marathon in her veins. Squirming on the inside, she suddenly wondered why she was even attempting to make a good impression on him.

After that moment, everything seemed hazy. Rhea asked him some questions and disinterestedly replied to the ones that he posed. Her mind snapped back to the present when she heard him say, 'So, are you interested in cooking-shooking?'

I'm still studying, silly, and I have my Board Exams this year, or didn't you know that already? Where's the time to learn how to cook? The rebel inside her wanted to scream out loud.

Rhea hated 'cooking-shooking' and it was always a sore topic of discussion for her. A woman's life didn't have to revolve around the kitchen! *Okay! Okay! Calm down! Breathe!*

'No, I don't know how to cook,' she replied curtly, not giving any further explanation. She gleefully thought that she'd given him another reason to say 'No'.

'I'm sure you'll learn eventually.' He sounded completely insouciant. *That was the typical Indian male way of thinking!* Rhea held her tongue and murmured, 'I guess so. Do you know how to cook?'

The 'are-you-crazy' look on his face was reward enough for her! Gotcha! The devil in her mind gave her a high-five.

'Well, no, I don't really know how to cook. I just know how to eat!' On hearing this, Rhea immediately deducted the brownie points that he had earned earlier on his handling of her juvenile virgin question.

'What are your views on marriage?' he asked her, appearing disappointed that Rhea didn't react to his joke the way he had expected her to.

'Well, I've not given it a serious thought until now, you know. This is all very new and sudden,' she answered, truthfully.

'Fair enough. But now that you are here, what are your thoughts? Are you willing to settle down in Delhi? What about your studies?' asked Happy with genuine concern on his face.

Wanting to sound mature for once, Rhea answered, 'I've not thought about moving to Delhi but I'm not averse to the idea. And before coming to meet you, my parents told me that if things work out, they would let me finish my graduation before the whole marriage thing happens. So I'm just playing it by ear.'

'There's always the option of studying in Delhi after marriage,' offered Happy prosaically. Rhea didn't know what was happening and how this conversation had become so definitive. This was not how it was supposed to be. She panicked.

'I guess,' she finally said then, after a pause, added, 'I think we should go out and join the others. They'll be wondering where we've disappeared.'

'Yeah, sure. If there's anything else that you want to ask me, feel free to do so,' he said.

Forcing a smile, she answered, 'No, there's nothing else.' Desperate to escape, she made a beeline for the door. However, her relief was short-lived. She now knew what being caught between the devil and the deep blue sea was like. As soon as they entered the drawing room, there was pin-drop silence and her discomfort touched new heights.

'So, how was it? Did you both get to know each other?' asked a lady immediately. That was his boisterous aunt, Pammi, Rhea would soon find out.

'Yes, we did, Pammi Aunty,' Happy came to her rescue. Rhea smiled at him and was about to grab the empty seat next to her father when Pammi caught hold of her hand and stopped her.

'You also come here, Happy.'

Rhea was confused. What Pammi did next embarrassed her to the very depths of her being. In full view of all the gathered relatives, she made Rhea and Happy stand side by side, taking a step backwards to look at them as if assessing something. Seeming satisfied, she spoke to Rhea. 'Rhea, can you wear your shoes and come back here please?' That was when Rhea realised what Pammi was doing. Apparently, the 'height check' test was in progress!

She dared not look in the direction of her mother. The platform heels she had worn in childish defiance were going to get her killed today. She slowly walked towards the main door where they had taken off their footwear. Gurleen's flat golden sandals caught her eye and she quickly wore them instead of her own shoes. *Thank God Mumma and I have the same foot size.*

When Rhea came back into the room, Pammi was waiting while Happy looked somewhat discomfited. This time Rhea met her mother's eyes confidently, knowing full well that she would be proud of her daughter's presence of mind.

When everyone was satisfied with the height check test that Pammi had conducted, Rhea heaved a sigh of relief. After a few more pleasantries and mundane talk, Mona beckoned Happy to another room.

Rhea took the opportunity to softly talk to her father. 'Please take me home. This is all so overwhelming. How could she check our height so blatantly in front of everyone? It was so embarrassing, Papa!'

'Relax, *beta*. Forget Pammi. Tell me what you guys talked about. Did you like him? Happy's parents seem to like you and they've asked us to stay in Delhi for another day so you both can spend some time with each other,' he whispered in a conspiratorial tone.

'What? When did this happen? Papa, you know, I'm going to miss school for two whole days. What about my exams?' muttered Rhea through clenched teeth. All she wanted was some time with her parents to speak her mind but they were stuck here with no way out, or so it seemed.

Just then, Happy and Mona re-entered the drawing room and any further hush-hush conversation with Jaspal was out of the question.

'Why don't the kids go out for a drive and get to know each other? Rhea will get to see Delhi also. We elders can relax at home,' suggested Mona.

Rhea had no choice but to smile politely and look at her parents for their go-ahead. She was slowly giving in to what lay in store for her. There was no running away from this and she thought that the sooner she accepted it, the better.

Amidst her turbulent thoughts, she could hear Jaspal giving his permission and someone else saying that Happy's cousins would be accompanying them on the drive.

So much for getting to know each other, thought Rhea, angrily, confused about why she was irritated rather than relieved that they weren't going alone. She wondered who these cousins were and how comfortable she would be with them. Hadn't she had her share of strangers today? Would they tease her and ask weird questions? The situation was that much more complicated because of the nonsense that came with 'arranged marriage'.

Once they were out, Rhea discovered that her inhibitions were totally unnecessary. These were a bunch of kids just like her and she was totally at ease as they showed her various Delhi landmarks, starting with India Gate in the heart of the city.

After an hour of driving around, Happy suggested they head back home and Rhea was a tad disappointed. She was having so much fun that for a moment she had forgotten why she was here. Her tension elevated as they reached his home again. But thankfully, the party of relatives had dispersed in their absence. Rhea couldn't wait to run to her parents.

She was told that they were resting in the guest room. When she walked in and saw the happy, expectant smiles on their faces, her heart sank.

2

Yes, We Do!

'So how was it? Did you like him? What did you talk about? Did you enjoy yourself? He seems like such a nice boy and the family is also very warm. I think it's the perfect match. What do you think?' Gurleen could not contain her enthusiasm.

'I think he's okay. How can I know for sure after spending such little time with him?' Rhea replied carefully, adding, 'and he is a bit short.'

'Oh, don't be silly. He's not short. This is the best thing that could have happened to us. You will be very happy here. They have already told us that they like you.'

'What? His family has already agreed? Did he tell his parents that he likes me? Now what? What did you tell them? Am I supposed to say 'Yes'? Are you going to get me engaged right away? What about the marriage? Did you tell them that I want to finish my studies?' Rhea's panic knew no bounds. Her comfy world was disintegrating and she was finding it harder and harder to breathe. She had to find a way out. 'I don't like him that much and besides, I want to study more,' she ranted.

'Jaspal*ji*, please make her understand. She doesn't know what she's saying. Happy is well-educated, well-mannered and well-settled. The family has a flourishing import-export business. It's very difficult to find so many good qualities in one person these days,' Gurleen appealed to her husband.

So far, Jaspal had been quiet, just listening to the verbal exchange between mother and daughter. 'Give her some time to settle down, Gurleen. We've all had a long and tiring day and there is no pressure on us to reply immediately.'

Rhea sat down on the bed next to him. Jaspal knew his daughter well and like all doting parents, also knew the right chords to strike. He gave his wife a 'You-stay-out-of-it-I'll-handle-it' look and spoke to Rhea. 'Don't worry. We are not putting any pressure on you. Just tell me what is on your mind.'

'I don't think I want to get married so early, Papa, and I'm not even sure if I like him. What about my studies? You are not answering any of my questions!' wailed Rhea, frustrated at repeating the same concerns yet again. Regardless of how nice the family was and the fact that Happy seemed like a decent boy, she was scared of what lay ahead. She didn't want to venture into that complicated arena of life so early. Her mother had married at the age of 19 and given birth to her when she was 21. Rhea didn't know what her own professional aspirations were yet, but she definitely didn't want to be slotted into a wife's role just yet!

Much to her displeasure, Jaspal began showing her the bright side: the handsome boy, the family, the comfort, the money, the name and many other pros. Rhea was slowly getting swayed, warming to the picture he was painting.

'He's their only son. Look at the advantage in that. You will be the apple of your in-laws' eyes and obviously his too. We want nothing but the best for you and if we had felt that there was something not right here then we would have said "No" ourselves. But this really is a match made in heaven,' said Jaspal.

Rhea snapped out of the magical world he had taken her into. She couldn't believe her ears. 'Made in heaven! My foot!'

Jaspal immediately reprimanded her with a stern look, which was rare. The bond between father and daughter was so strong that it could put many friendships to shame. Rhea was a bit taken aback at his expression, which now bordered on fury.

'Just look at her attitude! This is not going to get her anywhere in life,' said Gurleen.

'Look, Rhea, think about it overnight. This is a good thing; don't dismiss it for some silly reasons. We have to tell them our decision in the morning and you should know that he likes you,' said Jaspal, ignoring Gurleen's outburst.

With that, they retired for the night. Rhea was sleepless and hungry. She hadn't been able to eat much through the day and had avoided eating when they were out of the house. But she stubbornly refrained from asking her mother for dinner. Hungry and angry, she went to bed. But sleep evaded her. Tossing and turning on the floor mattress that had been laid in the same room her parents were in, she just couldn't fall asleep. After 15 minutes, she heard her parents snoring and knew that they were fast asleep.

'Oh, Papa! Stop snoring please!' Rhea wanted to shake him awake! She wondered if she should tiptoe out of the room.

They were on the 21st floor of the building. Jaspal had mentioned that theirs was the first and only high-rise residential complex in Delhi so far. Rhea had caught a glimpse of the balcony from where the view would surely be nothing but spectacular. She was seized with the urge to explore, and get some fresh air in the process. Straining her ears for any kind of sound outside, Rhea mustered up the courage to get out of the room and headed towards the balcony. Thankfully, the door opened without a squeak. She got out, took in the fresh air and gazed in awe at the view that lay before her.

The crescent moon was playing hide and seek with the clouds and Delhi was brightly lit up in various shades of yellow, white, red and blue, the colours of the private bungalows that surrounded the lone tall tower.

'It's beautiful, isn't it?'

Rhea jumped! Happy was quick to grab her and put his hand across her mouth before her scream woke up someone in the house.

'*Oye*! It's me. Don't scream. Sorry I startled you. I didn't expect to find you here at this hour,' he said, still holding her but having removed his hand from over her mouth.

Rhea's heart was racing. This was surreal. The light hum of traffic, the clouds embracing the moon's ethereal beauty and the height that they were at, dwarfing everything around them…it was dreamlike. Light-headed, she was suddenly feeling somewhat coquettish but had no idea what to say or do.

Then she became aware of his hand on her waist. Happy was looking at her strangely, a look which turned Rhea's knees to jelly. Suddenly, he moved away and composed himself.

'What are you doing out here so late? Couldn't sleep?' he asked.

'Yes, and I'm also very hungry,' replied Rhea, holding on to the balcony railing, not trusting her feet for support.

'Oh! Why didn't you eat anything? Come, let's find something in the kitchen,' he said.

Rhea followed him to the kitchen, praying that they didn't wake up anyone else. She didn't want to be seen alone with him in the middle of the night. God alone knew what his family would think of her! Her mother had told her time and again that a girl always had to be extra careful about her reputation. Gurleen's words—*your reputation always precedes you*—echoed in her mind.

While Rhea was deep in thought, Happy was scanning the fridge and opening containers. 'There's some butter chicken here. Would you like that?' he asked, his head inside the fridge.

'Not really,' Rhea said, overcome with shyness. 'Actually, let it be. I'll just go to sleep now. It's really okay.'

'But you must eat before you sleep. Should I make you some Maggi?' Happy offered.

'That would be excellent. But I can make it myself. Just tell me where the things are. Do you want some too?' Rhea managed to say despite her over-active state of mind.

'I'll probably take a bite or two from you, not more,' he said.

She cooked a packet of noodles sans any untoward or embarrassing incident and they sat down at the kitchen table to eat. One bowl, two forks! How had it come to this? This midnight rendezvous and the moment in the balcony were making Rhea's insides flutter! Did he feel it too? And hadn't her mother said that he liked her? That thought brought her back to reality.

Rhea found it difficult to say anything. She ate quietly, all the while feeling his eyes on her. *Say something*, she wanted to tell him but couldn't utter the words. They continued eating in silence. Once they had wiped the bowl clean, she got up to return to bed. 'I'll see you in the morning,' she said. 'Goodnight and thank you for the Maggi. It was a saviour.'

'The pleasure was mine. Goodnight and sweet dreams,' replied Happy with a sweet smile.

Her heart skipped a beat as she slowly turned and snuck back into the room where her parents were sleeping. She wore a stupid smile as she hid her face in the pillow. She couldn't fathom what was happening to her and why she was so happy all of a sudden. Now she couldn't even say the word 'happy' without thinking about him. 'Happy Singh!' Rhea sighed.

While she was still going over the events of the last few minutes, the day's fatigue gradually caught up with her and she drifted off to sleep.

'Good morning! It's almost eight o'clock! Let's get ready and go for breakfast.' Gurleen's voice woke her up.

Rhea could have caught another 40 winks before getting out of bed but instead she smiled at her mother. Gurleen gave her a confused look but smiled back nonetheless. 'Come on, get up,' she said again and Rhea sat up almost immediately. Heading to the bathroom for a shower, she asked, 'Can I wear jeans?'

'Yes, of course,' replied Gurleen, giving Jaspal a quizzical look. As long as she was not resisting, sulking or getting angry, it was going to be okay, they thought.

Rhea emerged from the bathroom 15 minutes later, dressed in her jeans and a white T-shirt. Brushing her hair, she asked her mother the plan for the day.

'Let's step outside and we'll know the plan. Have you decided what your answer is going to be? Remember that this is a great proposal,' said Gurleen, not wanting to be too pushy.

'If you think it's best for me, then I don't have a problem. I just wish I had some more time to think about it,' said Rhea, confidently.

Her parents could not believe what they'd just heard. Rhea could see how happy her acceptance had made them and she felt good about it while trying to ignore the fact that they had turned a deaf ear to her plea for time.

'That's our girl. You will be so happy here. Come on, if you're ready, we should go out for breakfast. They've already called us once,' said Gurleen.

Rhea was nervously happy. Or was it happily nervous? The previous night kept playing on her mind. Looking fresh and pretty, Rhea stepped into the dining room with her parents. Happy's parents and his cousin Neetu, who had accompanied them on the drive last night, were deep in conversation at the dining table when they entered. Happy was missing.

Where is he? thought Rhea as she said her *Sat Sri Akal*s and 'good mornings' to the family.

'Neetu, will you please call Happy? I think he's getting ready,' Mona told her niece.

'These boys, I tell you, sometimes they take more time to get ready than girls. I'll go get him,' Neetu chirped and went to call Happy.

After some idle chatter at the breakfast table, Happy's father, Satvinder, addressed her. 'So, Rhea, how did you like our family? I hope you enjoyed your stay here.'

'Yes, uncle, thank you so much. I've had a nice time and your family is wonderful. It was fun going around Delhi last evening since this is my first visit to the city,' she replied with such poise that she surprised herself. Gurleen beamed with pride and Jaspal had a huge grin on his face.

Mona took over the conversation. 'I'm glad you enjoyed yourself. We hope you've had some time to get to know Happy. From our side, we will be very happy to have you as our daughter-in-law.'

Rhea could feel her face turning red as blood rushed to her cheeks. She looked at her father for some respite from this situation. From the corner of her eye, she could see Happy enter the room.

'Actually, we were so tired last night that we didn't really get the time to ask her about it,' said Jaspal, realising that there were some things he needed to discuss with Rhea before they gave a formal answer.

'That's understandable. Please take your time. There's no hurry. We thought that if both families agree, we could do a small informal *roka* ceremony before you all left,' said Mona.

'Yes, of course. Give us some time to talk to Rhea and we'll get back to you,' replied Gurleen, confused with her husband's reply but falling in step nonetheless.

Rhea might as well have been invisible. They were talking about her as if she wasn't even sitting at the table. Would it be preposterous to ask if she could talk to Happy alone once before giving her reply?

'Rhea, if you've finished your breakfast, let me show you the view from the balcony. It's beautiful in the mornings and you can see a big chunk of Delhi from this height,' said Happy.

She looked at him wide-eyed, not believing what he'd just suggested. Not that he had said anything wrong. In fact, wasn't she just thinking about getting some time alone with him? And here he had read her mind. She couldn't help but feel self-conscious.

'Oh, really! That would be nice,' replied Rhea, aware that once again, they were the centre of attention.

Once alone, Happy told her, 'I hope I didn't embarrass you but it looked like you needed to get out of there.'

'You've been my knight in shining armour,' Rhea blurted out without thinking and was immediately embarrassed at what she'd said. He laughed a genuine laugh and with that, her foot-in-mouth remark faded into oblivion.

'You are so filmy! But jokes apart, I wanted to talk to you without the elders being around. I didn't realise they would bring up the topic at breakfast. Being discreet isn't a family trait,' joked Happy.

Giving a small laugh, Rhea said, 'I wanted to talk to you too. Your parents said they've liked me and my parents have loved everything about you and your family. So now I guess it has been left to us!'

Rhea decided she would hear him out before saying anything else. Her worries—completing her studies, becoming a housewife at such an early age, not knowing how to cook, letting go of any career dreams, leaving her friends behind—were doing the samba in her head. *Shit! This is it. What am I going to say? What am I going to say? What am I going to say?*

'Well, I like you, your attitude and the way you carry yourself. You have a good sense of humour and you're honest about what you feel without twisting words. I like people who are straightforward. I think we would be good together. What do you think?' Happy delivered his spiel and, far too soon, the ball was back in her court.

She looked at him, smiled and began speaking, choosing her words carefully. 'It's been so sudden that I don't know what to say. You come across as a nice guy. But everything is happening very fast and I'm a little confused about what I really want,' replied Rhea, being as truthful as she could.

'I appreciate your honesty and there is no pressure on you to reply right away, despite what my mother may have said. Take some time to think,' Happy said.

With that, they headed back inside the house and joined the others. As soon as Rhea's parents saw her coming back, they excused themselves and asked her to join them in their room.

Rhea could feel her heart blowing hot and cold alternatively towards Happy and the entire situation. While she had woken up with a spring in her step, she was now feeling burdened with the life-altering decision she had to make. She addressed her parents as soon as they had closed the door behind them. 'What should I do? He's a nice guy and the family is also nice. But I never anticipated being in a situation like this at 15! I don't even know how to cook.'

'Getting worked up at this point is not going to help you make a decision, Rhea. Calm down and think rationally,' said Gurleen.

'Rationally? But isn't it irrational that you want me to get married at 15?' answered Rhea, exasperated.

'We told you there would be a courtship period. We are not getting you married right away. Don't get tense,' said Jaspal in a soothing tone. The patience card usually worked on his daughter.

'We need to give them an answer. You heard what they said and it's okay if you want to say "No". We were never holding a gun to your head, but you need to make up your mind,' said Gurleen, resorting to reverse psychology.

'You know I'm not saying "No,"' said Rhea, feeling guilty and giving her parents the response she knew they desired.

'It's alright. What did Happy tell you in the balcony?' Jaspal asked.

Rhea repeated their conversation.

'He comes across as an understanding boy. I think he will keep you happy,' said Gurleen and they all laughed.

'Happy better keep my daughter happy!' said Jaspal, trying to keep a check on his emotions even while laughing with them.

'He will! They're expecting us to give an answer in sometime. If we have to say "No", we should go out and tell them we need time to think and that we will reply in a couple of days once we're back home. That way we can avoid an uncomfortable situation,' suggested Gurleen.

'I told you, Mumma, I'm not rejecting him,' repeated Rhea.

'But you're not saying "Yes" either, *beta*,' said Jaspal.

'If you think this is the right thing for me, then I'm okay with it,' Rhea heard herself mouthing the same words she'd uttered in the morning but this time she knew better than to add the 'I-need-some-time' plea.

There was no looking back now. Her fate was sealed. 'Should I be happy or sad?' She thought and then smiled to herself. It looked like there was no escaping 'happy' now.

'You've made the right decision. We are so proud of you,' said Gurleen.

Those words pulled her out of the 'happy' zone. She wondered what feat she had accomplished to make her mother 'proud'. Was it a matter of pride that Rhea had agreed to get married at 15? There was no point mulling over it now. The decision was made and she couldn't back away. She'd do anything to be able to speak to

Aditi right now but her best friend was probably daydreaming in a classroom while the teacher droned on about pollen or something.

'Come on, let's go tell them the good news. I'm sure they are waiting,' said Gurleen, her joy knowing no bounds.

Rhea was lost as if in a trance. Her mother's ultimate happiness lay in the fact that her daughter was getting married into a good family to a nice boy. This was the quintessential Indian family value system that she was born into and there was no avoiding it. She was listening but not hearing, looking but not seeing. Jaspal watched his daughter with concern.

Rhea followed her parents outside, feeling a bit low. Her heart and mind were arguing. *But isn't it your own decision? No one forced you to say 'Yes'. Why are you sulking? He's a nice guy, good-looking too, and he likes you. Snap out of it.*

Telling herself to straighten up, Rhea decided she was ready to face the new world where, in a matter of moments, new familial connections would be thrust upon her: daughter-in-law, sister-in-law and fiancée. Rhea felt brave till she saw Happy waiting nervously for them. Her heart did a flip-flop. This was the boy who would be her husband. She could be happy with Happy, or so she kept telling herself.

'It will be an honour to give our daughter's hand in marriage to your family,' Jaspal told Satvinder, Happy's father, rather formally.

There was a flutter of activity all around and everyone was hugging each other. Rhea's eyes were glued to Happy's and she saw a promise in them, an assurance that everything was going to be just perfect!

But Rhea was *still* unsure.

3

Deal-breaker

'You're kidding! You're engaged? You should be thinking about your Board Exams but you've ended up getting engaged? Have you gone mad? How could you agree? You didn't even tell me anything before going to meet this guy. I was wondering where you'd disappeared when you didn't show up in school. Preet told me that you had gone to Delhi for some function. She didn't say it was *your* engagement! What are we going to do now?' Aditi was screaming at Rhea.

Rhea Khurrana and Aditi Grover had been inseparable ever since they had become best of friends a couple of years ago. All their critical life decisions were always taken together. Which tuition teacher to go to for extra classes? Which subject to study first? Which boy was cuter? Which movie to watch at the Gymkhana Club?

Aditi's yelling was justified because Rhea had not even thought it important to consult her best friend regarding this watershed moment in her life.

'Calm down, AG. Do you…' began Rhea.

'Don't AG me right now, Rhea Khurrana! You know I'm angry,' Aditi snapped, cutting her off.

Rhea realised that reasoning with Aditi was not going to work. She had to try a different tactic. Going to her mother's room, she returned shortly with a SkyBag.

While Aditi was sulking, Rhea opened the bag and slowly started removing its contents. She knew curiosity would get the better of her friend and they would be laughing and talking again in no time. She was right!

'What is all this? Did you go shopping in Delhi, you bitch? Did you buy anything for me?' said Aditi, coming closer to inspect the paraphernalia.

'No, silly, I didn't go shopping. These are gifts from my husband-to-be and his family,' Rhea said, failing to hide the pride in her voice.

There were Indian and Western clothes, diamond jewellery, bags, perfumes, clips, make-up, a limited edition Montblanc pen set and a cute and cuddly stuffed turtle dressed in vibrant shades of green, yellow, blue and purple.

'Let me see the jewellery. Whoa! Look at this heart-shaped diamond pendant. It's gorgeous. So now you're wearing his heart around your neck! This is exciting! What's his name? What does he do? How old is he? Is he handsome? Did you guys kiss? I want to know it all.' Aditi fired off a barrage of questions.

'Shhh. Shut up, Adu! We did no such thing. Control yourself. Let my mother not hear you.'

At 15, Rhea and Aditi had discussed what their first kiss and first boyfriend would be like. Of course, actually kissing a boy or going out with him was out of the question in Jalandhar. But that didn't deter the girls from dreaming.

'Can you imagine that I'm never going to have a boyfriend? I'm getting married straightaway. It's kind of scary.'

'Tell me about him, what happened, how did it happen? I want to know everything.'

Rhea recounted her time in Delhi.

'And don't you dare laugh at this but his name is…Happy!' Rhea had left the worst for last.

That did it for Aditi. She just couldn't control the bursts of laughter that followed and was rolling on the bed, hands clutching her stomach. And as Rhea joined her friend in making fun of his name, she knew everything would be alright!

'Happyyyyy! Unbelievable! Oh and have you thought how people would sing on his birthday? Happy birthday to you! Happy birthday to you! Happy birthday dear Happyyyyyy! Happy birthday to you!'

'I cannot believe you actually did this sing-song thing! And imagine if I have to do this on his birthday every year after we get married. God help me if I start laughing!'

'Oh, man!'

'Oh, forget about his name. Tell me what I should tell the girls in school. There's no way I can hide something like this for long,' Rhea said.

'There's no need for you to volunteer any information about this. If anyone asks you, just say that the marriage will not happen until you finish your studies here and then you will complete your graduation in Delhi. LSR is one of the best colleges there. How exciting that will be, *na*? Maybe then I can convince my parents to send me to Delhi too and we can study together! This is turning out to be awesome.'

'Oh shitttt!' Rhea suddenly shouted, startling Aditi.

'What now?'

'How am I going to tell the boys about this? They are going to have so much fun at my expense.'

'Relax, we will deal with those buffoons when the time comes,' Aditi reassured her.

'The Boys' were an integral part of their lives. Rhea, Aditi, Jaskaran, Anuj and Aadish were the thickest of friends. Jalandhar was a conservative town and the society at large looked down upon friendship between girls and boys. However, coming from a relatively broad-minded upper middle class family, Aditi's parents had no problems about boys being among her friends.

The same was not true for Rhea. Gurleen was strict and liked to keep her kids under control. Instead of forming a bond with her children, she had chosen to keep them under rigid vigilance. Nonetheless, Jaspal usually managed to compensate for his wife's tough exterior.

Given the fact that her mother didn't like her interacting with boys, Rhea's meetings with the gang were limited. They met once a week either at the Gymkhana Club or at Aditi or Aadish's house and on most of these occasions, Rhea confided in her father.

Before the trip to Delhi, the group had decided to meet during the weekend, which was now two days away. Rhea was glad that she had some time in hand before facing them. While she was lost in her thoughts, Aditi was checking out all the new clothes that were now a part of Rhea's closet.

At that moment, the twins walked in. 'So you're showing off all your new things,' said Preet, the slightly older twin.

'Twinsters! Bug me not. Go away,' said Rhea.

'Give me one of these pens *na*. You know I've just started writing with pens in school and Mom will never buy me such a good-looking one. You have two of them!' said Geet, eyeing the expensive set.

'If you give her one, you have to give me the other. I prefer the ink pen,' Preet butted in.

'Don't even think about it. Now leave us alone or I'll complain,' Rhea threatened. The twins made a face and left. With three years separating Rhea from them, they were a bit young to understand what was going on in their elder sister's life.

Once they left, Aditi apprised her of the weekend plan and then left for home.

It had hardly been a day since their return from Delhi but Rhea's thoughts continued to revolve around Happy. After the informal engagement ceremony, the two of them had gone out for a drive. The most they'd done was hold hands when they stopped at a Gurudwara to seek blessings.

Rhea wondered when they would meet again. She was in love with the mere idea of being in love. She had had a couple of crushes before but nothing serious. Now, finally, she had someone around whom she could weave her dreams. She didn't know if it was possible to fall in love with anyone so soon but her child-like heart thrived in a make-believe world.

The weekend came and went and the boys were not as cruel to her in their jokes as she had imagined they would be. After expressing initial shock and disbelief, they recovered and carried on in their usual ways.

Time seemed to fly and Rhea was happy. The mammoth engagement ring that she had found very heavy in the initial days of her engagement had now become a comfortable daily accessory on her finger. Of course, she always remembered to slip it off when she went to school.

Happy used to call her once a week on the landline. She would wait eagerly for his call but they had to follow protocol; first, her parents would talk to his parents and then Jaspal would talk to him. Rhea would sometimes have to wait for almost 20 minutes before finally being handed the phone.

It had been five months since the engagement and their phone conversations would mostly revolve around the events of the week gone by. Since Rhea was still studying and a minor, there had been no discussions about setting a date for the wedding from either family. Meanwhile, she had given her ICSE exams and was confident about her performance despite the major distraction in her life. She passed with flying colors. To complete the two years of Junior College, Aditi and Rhea had changed schools and applied for admission in St. Joseph's School, where the boys were studying.

Aadish didn't attend Junior College as he was due to leave for Delhi as a result of his father's transfer. Soon, their gang of five would be one short. However, till the time he was in town, he would come to meet them every day after school.

The big discussion in the group now revolved around Aadish's farewell party. Rhea knew she would never get permission to attend it. She looked crestfallen just thinking about all the fun she would miss out on.

'What are you doing sitting here alone like this? Is something wrong?' Aditi spotted her and got right to the point, sensing Rhea's melancholic mood.

'You know I won't get permission for Aadish's farewell party. Lady Hitler will never allow me and I'm scared to even ask her. I can't believe I'm going to miss it.'

'Why don't you tell her that you're spending the night with me? Come over; we'll get ready and go for the party from my house. That way she won't get to know anything and you don't even need to ask for permission.'

Aditi had a solution for every problem. 'Now that we're sorted on that front, tell me, what are you planning to wear?'

That discussion cheered up Rhea instantly.

Two days later, she was carefully packing her overnight bag, constantly looking over her shoulder to make sure Gurleen didn't walk in on her and see the dress she was taking along. Before leaving, she reminded her mother that Aditi's phone was dead and that she would be back home by noon the next day.

Aditi and her younger sister, Devika, were getting ready when Rhea reached. 'Hiii! Get ready quickly. Mom and Dad are leaving for dinner in 10 minutes and they'll drop us to Aadish's house. I've told Mom that one of the boys will drop us back.'

'That's great. I'll be ready in five,' Rhea replied.

'How am I looking? I've put some make-up. Is it too much? Should I remove it?' rattled off Aditi while putting on her earrings.

Devika butted in. 'You look like a slut! Remove that shit from your cheeks and lighten that lipstick.'

Aditi smacked her sister and told her to shut up.

'You two don't start a fight now. Just lighten your lipstick a bit and make it subtle. The rest is fine. Don't worry about it. There will be some "seniors" at the party too and of course you want to look good in front of them,' said Rhea, winking at her friend.

Aditi's heart flip-flopped every time she saw Shrey, who was a year senior to them. Though they would sometimes talk casually, only Rhea and Devika knew that she was harbouring a major crush on him and imagined herself to be in love.

Aadish's farewell party was a super success and while alcohol was flowing freely, Rhea and Aditi refrained from drinking. The girls had promised Aditi's mother, Nita, that they would have their first glass of alcohol with her when they turned 18.

The next morning, when Rhea entered her house, she immediately sensed that something was wrong. She saw her mother crying copious tears in the drawing room while her father and some of his cousins were in a deep discussion.

Shit! Did someone pass away? Rhea thought the worst. It was tough to make her mother cry!

'What happened, Mumma? Why are you crying?'

All eyes in the room were on her. It was as if they had been waiting for her to arrive. Yet, no one spoke.

'Why are you all looking at me like this? What happened? Why is Mumma crying?'

'Happy's father called this morning to say that they're no longer interested in the marriage,' Jaspal told Rhea.

'What?' Rhea's heart began pounding. 'Did they tell you why?'

'They told us that Happy was not interested anymore. He didn't give any specific reason. Do you know what might have happened?' asked Jaspal.

'No, Papa. But it's not the end of the world. Is it? Maybe this is a blessing. Everything happens for a reason.' Rhea didn't know what else to say but she knew she had to be strong. The enormity of the news had not yet sunk in.

'Do you understand the repercussion this is going to have on your life?' asked one of her older uncles.

'Maybe I don't but there's nothing we can do about it. We're not going to plead in front of them now, are we?' answered Rhea, feeling bold. Her heart was beating fast and her palms were sweaty. She was feeling uneasy.

In her heart of hearts, Rhea knew that one little prank at Aadish's party the previous night might have resulted in Happy calling off their engagement. *How unsporting of him to take a harmless phone call so seriously without even giving her a chance to explain!* But she didn't have the courage to say anything to anyone right now. She would be royally screwed if she even attempted to explain what had happened. The guilt was slowly gnawing at her insides, a sense of dread clouding her thinking process. The fact that this development had made her parents terribly upset traumatised her. At this point, Rhea was, unable to fathom the repercussions this would have on her life. She tried hard to wipe that thought out from her mind and forced herself to focus on the brighter side: her studies, college, career. There was a whole new life in front of her now with a million possibilities.

Over the next five-six weeks, Gurleen was visibly upset that her daughter's engagement had been called off, whereas Jaspal tried his best to stay strong and appear unperturbed by the development. Rhea took some time to get over Happy and their 'happily ever after' that was now not to be. She wasn't sure whether it had been love or a mere acceptance of the situation that she had found herself in. However, little did Rhea know that the innocent tryst with Happy would come back to haunt her repeatedly for the better part of her adult life.

4

Blooming Puppy Love

The news of her broken engagement spread across Jalandhar like wildfire. Her parents retreated into their shells and turned down every invitation that came their way for the next couple of months. They were in no mood to socialise and answer questions that would inevitably be asked by obnoxious acquaintances.

On the other hand, Rhea had no choice but to go about her normal routine. She could neither avoid her friends nor could she stay out of school. If someone did ask her what happened, she explained that she didn't know the exact reason the boy's family had called off the engagement.

Aditi and Rhea avoided discussing Happy. They both knew it was a topic that was best laid to rest. They had implicitly agreed to let bygones be bygones.

Despite being strong on the outside, Rhea's mind and heart were often in turmoil. It was not as if she was totally unaffected by the events that had taken place. Her first year of Junior College was almost coming to an end and there had been a marked change in Rhea's behaviour since the unforeseen event. She was subdued and avoided parties, lying low in her parents' eyes. They never blamed her for what had happened but guilt was eating away at her.

Meanwhile, there had been an addition to the group after Aadish left for Delhi: Rohan Shroff. Besides being the best-looking boy in their batch, he was also Anuj's close buddy. Since both of them hung out together most of the time playing basketball, Rohan would inevitably end up spending a lot of time with the rest of the group too. Slowly and without any formal induction, Rohan became a part of the gang.

Rhea was a bit shy in front of him, whereas Aditi was her usual gregarious self, totally unaffected. His good looks, self-confidence, charm and slightly bratty behaviour gave Rhea the heebie-jeebies. Scared that she would fall for his charm, she avoided him as much as she could. She didn't want any complication in her life right now.

Rhea and Rohan had met at a few birthday parties she had attended with Aditi. Sitting alone under the big Banyan tree outside the school canteen, Rhea's mind went into flashback mode to Shaila's party the previous year, when she had still been dreaming of her marriage with Happy. It was the first dance party that Rhea and Aditi had ever attended. Rohan had been there too.

Rhea remembered how she was a bundle of nerves when she showed up that evening. The 'mood lighting' in Shaila's drawing room made her heart skip a beat. This had been the first party Rhea had attended after she was engaged and she wasn't particularly interested in any of the boys around. She was standing in one corner talking to Anuj when, out of the blue, Rohan walked up to them. 'May I have the pleasure of this dance?'

Rhea blushed and looked at Anuj but he was already chatting up another girl nearby. She cursed him for leaving her alone. Rhea couldn't imagine why Rohan wanted to dance with her. Didn't he know that she was already engaged? She declined politely. 'I don't really know how to dance.' Her heart was hammering against her ribs so hard that she was scared he'd hear it.

'Oh, come on! There's nothing to it. Just follow my lead and it won't be difficult. I promise,' he insisted.

Not wanting to be rude, Rhea obliged. As soon as they got onto the dance floor, the music changed to a slow number as if by design.

Play!
Lay a whisper on my pillow,
Leave the winter on the ground.
I wake up lonely, there's air of silence
In the bedroom and all around
Touch me now, I close my eyes…

Rhea panicked. Shit! *Close dancing with Rohan and that too on 'It Must've Been Love'. A sureshot recipe for disaster.* She frantically looked around for Aditi and found her starry-eyed in the arms of Shrey, who had finally asked her for a dance.

She had no choice but to fall in step with Rohan while Roxette crooned softly in the background. She loved the way he was holding her, trying to be careful not to touch her too familiarly, yet securing her to him on the crowded dance floor. She felt a sense of guilty belonging and was at the risk of losing herself in his arms until he said, 'I hear you're engaged?'

Alert, Rhea straightened herself in his arms and put a little distance between them. 'Yes, you've heard right,' she smiled.

'When's the wedding? Will you invite me?' he teased, pulling her slightly closer.

Rhea was confused. She had never been in a situation like this before and didn't know how to react. She was thinking of an answer when Rohit Khanna, Rohan's friend and a senior from school, interrupted them.

'Come on, Rohan, you can't have this gorgeous girl to yourself all evening. Let me have the pleasure of dancing with her too,' Rohit said.

'She's all yours.' Rohan moved slightly away from her. 'Thank you for the lovely dance, Rhea, and have a happy life,' he told her.

'What was that all about?' Rohit asked her. Rhea didn't know where he had come from but was nevertheless glad of the reprieve. Shaila had briefly introduced her to Rohit outside one of her tuition classes a few months ago. Apart from that, she had never interacted with him directly, let alone in such close proximity.

'Thank you for that, but I didn't need rescuing. Did I look like a damsel in distress to you?' Rhea said, half-joking, feeling a little more confident than she had been when Rohan was around.

Rohit burst out laughing. 'Far from it, but I know this boy. He can be intimidating sometimes so I thought I'd be your knight in shining armour.'

Was he flirting with her? Rhea knew Rohit was seeing her classmate, Payal. He couldn't be flirting with her while his girlfriend was also at the party! Maybe he was genuinely concerned. They finished the rest of the dance in silence. She took his leave, thanking him once again.

Rohan, who found her sitting under the Banyan tree, broke into her thoughts, cutting short her reminiscing and bringing her back to the present.

'Thinking about me?'

Rhea blushed furiously and Rohan continued, unaware of where her mind had wandered.

'I've been looking all over for you and here you are, sitting under this tree and daydreaming. Where were you lost?'

Rhea ignored his question. 'What's up? Where are the others? I'm waiting for Aditi so we can go home.'

'She was looking for you and was getting late for a lunch she had to attend with her parents. She asked me to tell you that she was leaving with Jaskaran,' replied Rohan.

'She left without me? She was supposed to drop me home. How am I going to go now? Did they just leave? Maybe if I hurry, I can catch them outside,' Rhea blabbered on.

'Actually, they left 10 minutes ago. I went to the library first to look for you. I didn't think I would find you here. But I can drop you home if you want. I've got my Dad's car today,' Rohan offered.

Rhea had no option but to go along with him. Her house was 15 minutes away from school and there was an uncomfortable silence in the car. Rhea had always been careful not to be alone with Rohan but this was one situation she couldn't have avoided. She was still embarrassed that he had found her sitting under the tree at the same time she had been thinking about him.

Fingers twisted together in her lap, Rhea chose to look out of the window. From the corner of her eye, she could feel Rohan's eyes on her time and again. Her mind was in upheaval and she didn't know why.

'Are you okay, sweetheart?'

Rhea's eyes welled up. He held her hand and she couldn't stop her tears.

'Shhh, baby! Are you alright? Why are you crying? Come, let's go to the Gymkhana Club. Anuj might be there too.'

He didn't wait for an answer and she let him make the decision. Rhea didn't know why she was crying. How could Aditi leave her alone and go home? No sooner had this thought come to her mind that she wanted to laugh. This was childish. Why was she crying, and that too in front of Rohan?

He turned into the parking lot of the club. It was early afternoon and the place was almost deserted. They didn't get out of the car immediately and Rhea was suddenly self-conscious. She wiped away her tears and tried to compose herself.

Rohan turned around in his seat and took her face in his hands. 'What happened, baby? Why are you crying like this?'

That led to even more tears! Oh, why did he have to be so sweet and good-looking? And why was he calling her 'baby'?

He pulled her closer, wiped her tears away and put her head on his chest. She could hear his pounding heart. His lips on her forehead were sending tingling sensations down her spine. His hands were gently caressing her hair and he was mumbling sweet nothings to her.

Rhea's lips were lightly resting against the open V of his chest. She wanted to kiss him. Rohan moved her away from him slightly and his mouth found hers. Hardly had their lips touched when they heard a familiar bike horn. Guiltily, they jumped apart.

'Shit! It's Anuj and Shekhar. I'll get out and engage them in a conversation. You compose yourself and come out.'

Rohan called out to the boys and walked a little further away from the car and started talking to them. Rhea quickly wiped her tears and came up to them.

'What's wrong with you? Has he made you cry?' One look at her and Anuj knew Rhea had been crying.

'Oh no, don't be silly. It's nothing. I'm okay now, just feeling a bit low for no reason. Rohan was dropping me home and then we decided to come here looking for you,' replied Rhea.

'Chill out, darling. Let's go inside and have some omelette sandwiches. My stomach is complaining that I don't feed it enough.'

'Yeah! We all know that this Baby Elephant needs to be fed every hour. Let's go,' Rhea nudged him with her elbow.

She avoided looking directly at Rohan and instead made polite conversation with Shekhar, while Anuj gobbled up two plates of egg sandwiches and one plate of *pakoda*s.

When they finished eating, Shekhar went to the Club's library to issue a book. In his absence, Rohan said, 'I was thinking of a get-together at my place this weekend, just for our group. My parents aren't going to be home.'

Anuj said he was game and Rhea knew Aditi and Jaskaran would also agree.

'Will you be able to come, Rhea? Let's meet in the morning at my place and you girls can get home by evening before your curfew,' said Rohan as he gently took her hand in his under the table, quietly appealing to her to say yes.

'Shouldn't be a problem but I'll speak to Aditi and let you know,' replied Rhea.

Just then, Shekhar came back and the topic was closed.

Rohan dropped Rhea home. The drive back was without incident but there was a heavy silence in the air. She was still in two minds. Should she tell Aditi what had happened? She decided to hold on to her secret for some more time.

That night, Rhea couldn't sleep. She kept playing out the kiss-that-almost-was in her head and the sensations that Rohan's touch had stirred up inside her. Was she falling in love with him? Had she avoided him for so long due to this very fear? Ever since Shaila's birthday last year, Rhea had been overtly aware of his presence every time he was close to her. And now she could hardly believe that they had shared a romantic moment.

The consequences of falling in love with Rohan were looming large in her mind but she didn't want to focus on those thoughts. At that moment, all she cared about was dreaming up different scenarios in her mind about how they would spend the day at his house. Strange and unknown feelings were erupting in her brain and she couldn't wait to see him again.

5

Of Hugs, Kisses, Teddies and Tears

'You never ever take so much time to get ready, Rhea. Look at all these clothes on the bed. We're just going to Rohan's house. Will you hurry up? Jaskaran has been waiting for us down the road for the last 10 minutes,' shouted Aditi.

'Shhhhh…can you not announce to the whole world where we're going? I've told Mumma that we're going to Aanchal's place.'

'Why don't you tell her we're going to Rohan's?'

'I don't want to complicate things. She'll ask me a thousand questions. You know how she is. It's just better not to tell her.'

Rhea was nervous. She was dying to tell Aditi about what had happened between her and Rohan but decided to wait for an opportune moment. That little tryst was also responsible for the guilt she was feeling, which is why she didn't want to tell her mother anything.

They reached Rohan's place after half an hour. It was a beautiful house, which had been bought by his father—a hotshot lawyer in Jalandhar—just six months ago. The five of them settled down in the terrace garden, enjoying the afternoon sun, especially delightful in the winter chill.

Rhea saw Aditi and Jaskaran standing in one corner of the terrace, talking with their heads close together, and wondered what was cooking. Rohan looked comfortable in the garden chair and Rhea began imagining what it would be like to hold his hand right then. If this were a Bollywood movie, there would've been a song playing in the background.

Play!
Chaahe tum kuchh na kaho
Maine sunn liya
Ki saathi pyaar ka mujhe chun liya
Chun liya
Maine sunn liya
Pehla nasha
Pehla khumaar
Naya pyaar hai, naya intezaar
Kar loon main kya apna haal
Aye dil-e-bekaraar
Mere dil-e-bekaraar

...but Rhea's *'dil-e-bekaraar'* moment came to an abrupt end when Rohan interrupted her thoughts. 'I'm going to get a Thums Up. Do you want to come with me? It's getting hot here now. We can move downstairs if that's okay,' asked Rohan.

'Let's go. I don't mind getting a cold drink,' she replied.

'Guys, we're going downstairs. See you there,' Rohan shouted out to Aditi and Jaskaran but both of them were lost in their own conversation.

She followed Rohan downstairs and found Anuj chattering away and smiling into the phone. They decided to leave him alone and went into the kitchen. Once they were inside, she couldn't hold her questions in any longer. 'Is he having a scene with someone? Those two upstairs are also so into each other and I have no idea what's happening between them. Aditi is supposed to be my best friend. How did I miss all this?'

Pouring out the cola in two glasses, Rohan handed one to her. 'Do you want to see my room? We can talk there and I can tell you what you missed out on.'

Rohan didn't wait for her answer and began walking towards his room, which was towards the far end of the house. Rhea followed him, glass in hand. They entered his room and, much to her surprise, he locked the door behind them. 'Why have you locked the door? Open it right now. These guys might come looking for us and I don't want them to find it locked. What will they think?'

'No one is going to come looking for us for the next half hour at least and I locked the door because ever since the other day, I've been wanting to do this...'

Rohan put their glasses on the bedside table and pinned her against the wall, holding her hands firmly by her side. Captive against his strong body, Rhea was barely able to move. His scent was intoxicating and her knees were turning weak. With her wide-open eyes, she saw his face coming closer. He kissed her nose, eyes and cheeks one by one; then, very slowly, he put his lips on hers. Rhea shut her eyes and was lost in the depths of his sweet kiss.

Just when things were getting too steamy for her to handle, Rohan took her hand in his and looked at her earnestly. It took her breath away.

'Ever since we danced at Shaila's birthday party last year, I haven't been able to take my mind off you. It was so frustrating for me to know that you were engaged but that didn't stop me from wanting to be with you. I just didn't know what to do about it.'

Rohan was pouring his heart out to her. Was this really happening? Rhea was silent. She didn't know how to react.

'I love you, Rhea. Will you be my girlfriend?'

She wanted to say something but words had left her. All she could manage to do was nod. He took her in his arms again and this time their kiss was even more passionate. Rhea had never felt so secure before. She wanted to hold on to him forever.

'Why were you crying that day, baby?'

Rhea stiffened in his arms. She had never had a conversation with Rohan that involved her feelings. She didn't want to go there right now so she decided to answer with a question of her own. 'First tell me what's happening in the group and why I don't know anything.'

'There's definitely something happening between Aditi and Jaskaran but neither of them have come out and said so. They've been spending a lot of time together. I always knew Jaskaran liked her and it seems he recently told her so.'

'Bitch hasn't told me anything about it.'

'Language, my lady!' said Rohan, feigning shock, and they laughed as he kissed the sides of her lips. Rhea held him at arm's length. 'No more touching and kissing. Now tell me what perfume you're wearing. It's driving me crazy. Then tell me who Anuj is talking to.'

'It's D&G Cologne and I'm glad it's driving you crazy. Anuj is talking to Rachel. She's from your school. But you know him, he flirts with everything wearing a skirt. I don't know how serious he is about her.'

'Hmmm. I think I've been wallowing in self-pity all this while. I feel stupid not to have seen all this happening around me. They're my closest friends.'

Someone was trying to open the door from outside and Rohan went to unlock it. Rhea swiftly moved to his bookshelf and picked up the first book she saw: Sidney Sheldon's latest, *Nothing Lasts Forever*. She had no idea that the book's title was going to be an apt summation of her love life for the future.

Pretending to read the synopsis, she casually looked towards the door when Aditi and Jaskaran walked in. 'Why did you guys lock the door? What have you been upto?' Aditi looked extremely suspicious.

'Just talking and browsing through Rohan's books. I'm going to borrow this one for sure. Where have you been?'

'Why was the door locked, Rohan? Is there something we need to know?' Aditi ignored Rhea, knowing very well that she was being lied to.

'First, you both tell us what you have been doing. I might have been a little preoccupied lately to notice anything.' Rhea got straight to the point.

'We're in love with each other,' said Aditi without a pause. 'I've been dying to tell you but didn't know how to.'

'Oh My God! Really? How did I miss this? Since when has it been going on? Why didn't you tell me anything? I am so happy for both of you. Does Anuj know?'

Aditi told them excitedly that no one else knew and that the romance between them was hardly two weeks old. The best friends hugged. Jaskaran and Rohan joined them to make it a group hug.

'Well, we also have something to tell you guys. I'm in love with Rhea and I've just asked her out. Though she hasn't given me a proper answer, I'm pretty certain it's a yes!' Rohan informed the new couple.

'Ohmygod! Bitch! When did this happen? You've been hiding things from me?' exclaimed Aditi.

Rohan and Rhea looked at each other with a knowing smile. Looking at Aditi, they said in unison, 'Language, my lady!'

Hearing all the commotion, Anuj came to Rohan's room wanting to know what all the excitement was about. They apprised him of the recent developments in their lives and Anuj knocked the wind out of them with a shocker of his own. 'I've just asked Rachel out and she said "Yes". Can you believe it? She agreed! It's weird how all of us are suddenly in relationships.'

'You asked her out over the phone? That's ridiculous,' said Jaskaran.

'So what? It was pretty romantic,' insisted Anuj.

The chitter-chatter went on for some time and it was soon time for the girls to get back home. But Rhea did not want to leave Rohan. She wanted some alone time with him.

'I'll see you at St. J's on Monday.' Rohan made it sound like a promise, holding her tight.

~

The next few months flew by with their love affairs blossoming. The two couples tried to spend as much time with each other as possible without attracting too much attention.

Rhea did not publicly display her affection towards Rohan, not telling anyone they were dating. She had to be careful because if word got to her family, God alone knew what would happen.

In a week, Rhea was to travel to Surinder Mama's house in Bombay, now called Mumbai. This was the first time she wasn't looking forward to going to the city. Going there for one month meant being away from Rohan for that long and she couldn't even bear to think about it.

The evening before she was to leave, she went for a drive with him. Rhea was carrying her Sony walkman along with a blank cassette. They had decided that would record his voice so she could hear him and feel closer to him while they were apart.

Kabhi Kabhi was one of the most romantic songs that Hindi cinema had ever churned out and Rohan had promised he would sing it for her since it was their favourite.

Record!
Kabhi kabhi, mere dil mein, khayaal aata hai,
Ki jaise tujhko banaya gaya hai mere liye.
Tu abse pehle sitaaron mein bas rahi thi kahin,
Tujhe zameen pe bulaya gaya hai mere liye!

After he sang the entire song for her while driving, Rhea asked him to stop the car in one of the less busy lanes of Jalandhar. As soon as he halted at a secluded corner, Rhea launched herself on him and hugged him tight. Her eyes brimmed with tears. 'I'm going to miss you. I don't want to go to Bombay. I love you so much, baby!'

'What did you just say?'

'What?'

'You said you love me. Do you know this is the first time you've said it? I've been so sick of hearing "Ditto" every time I said I love you.'

They continued to hug as if Rhea was going to war and they were unsure if she would ever return!

The train journey from Jalandhar to Mumbai was hell. She kept listening to the song he had recorded for her and cried copious tears on the upper berth. He was singing for her and all she wanted to do was be with him forever.

Play! Stop! Rewind!

Play! Stop! Rewind!

When the walkman's battery got drained with all the constant rewinds and plays, she took out a spare set. When those too were on the verge of giving up, she resorted to using a pencil to manually rewind the tape again and again so she could keep hearing his voice. The pain of separation made Rhea realise how much she loved Rohan. He was her first love and would always remain special. She could not imagine life without him.

6

New Fish in a Bigger, Better Pond

'Babes, come to my house and spend the night. Let's finish studying the remaining history chapters and those scary Hindi poems. You know how much I suck at both,' Aditi was telling Rhea over the phone. They decided to go ahead with this plan the next day.

While Rhea was packing her overnight bag the following afternoon to go to Aditi's place, she thought about her miserable vacation. She had pined for Rohan and neither her mother nor her relatives could figure out what was bothering her. Even the always-mischievous twins hadn't changed her melancholic mood. When they had finally come back home from the vacation two weeks ago, no one was happier than her. Coming back to Jalandhar and to Rohan had been the best thing ever. However, they now had to begin studying for their preliminary exams, which were just a month away. The teachers had completed their respective syllabus and it was now optional for them to attend classes at St. J's. This limited Rhea's meetings with Rohan but they managed to meet at the club once a week and chatted on the phone whenever Rhea's mother was busy with her multiple social engagements.

That day, Rhea reached Aditi's place just in time for dinner. They decided to eat first and then study. Each had given their respective boyfriends a certain time for their midnight phone rendezvous but before that they had to finish studying a certain part of the syllabus. This pattern repeated itself over the next few weeks; the two girls were immersed in their books and studying together almost every alternate day. The boys, on the other hand, tried to replicate their model of combined studies but failed miserably.

Rhea and Aditi passed the preliminaries with flying colours and if their scores were any indication of the way they would perform in the Board Exams, there would be nothing to stop them from getting admission anywhere they wanted. Unlike the rest of their batchmates, who were hoping to get admission in Delhi's prestigious colleges like Lady Shri Ram, St. Stephen's, Shri Ram College of Commerce, Miranda House and Delhi College of Engineering, Rhea and Aditi's ultimate dream was to study in St. Xavier's College, Mumbai.

The immense pressure of studying did not get in the way of Rohan and Rhea's love life. It sometimes surprised Rhea that her parents had not yet got a whiff of her romantic liaison. But maybe she shouldn't have questioned the way things were going because it wasn't long before all hell broke loose.

'Will you come out for a drive with me in half an hour?' Rohan asked her over the phone one evening.

Rhea was moving around the house with the cordless phone and keeping an eye on her family members to keep from getting caught. Her father had just come home and was at the dining table, being served food. As long as he was eating, she could talk to Rohan.

'How can I? You know everyone is home, baby. There's no way I can get out.'

'Please, just for 10 minutes. I really want to see you.'

'No, Rohan! What will I say at home? It's way too risky.'

Suddenly, Rhea heard some static on the line. She slowly walked towards her parents' room where the landline extension was kept. She froze at the sight that greeted her.

Gurleen was listening in on her conversation. Rhea's heartbeat accelerated. She had no idea how long her mother had been on the extension. She disconnected the call as her mother put the phone back in place. She prayed that Rohan would not call her back.

Gurleen's look was thunderous. Rhea now knew the true meaning of the expression 'If looks could kill.'

'Who is he?'

Rhea could feel that this was a 'calm before the storm' question.

'Just a friend from school.'

'Just a friend? Where does he want to take you? What is going on between the two of you? Have you no shame? How long has this been going on? Jaspal*jiiiiii*!'

Hearing Gurleen's shrill scream, Jaspal rushed to the room, wondering what had happened.

'Ask her who Rohan is and what she has been talking to him about. What will happen if someone finds out? Is it not enough that her engagement has broken once? Now she's having an affair with another boy!'

Ouch! That was so below the belt! Rhea thought. *To hell with the broken engagement, and Rohan was definitely not a random boy!*

But there was no way she could muster up the courage to say anything in her defence. She chose to stand there submissively, taking in the verbal assault. After all, Gurleen wouldn't keep shouting all night long and Jaspal would definitely bail her out of this mess.

'Rohan is her friend from school. I remember her telling me about him. Isn't he Advocate Shroff's son? Anyway, what's wrong? Can someone please tell me what has happened?' Jaspal was perplexed.

Gurleen brought him up to speed with what she had heard and her anger reached boiling point just recounting that small portion of Rhea's conversation. At one point, when Rhea wasn't replying to any of her questions, Gurleen menacingly moved towards her and would have slapped her hard had Jaspal not stopped her just in time.

Rhea was familiar with being slapped. When they were younger, Gurleen spoke to Rhea, Preet and Geet with her hands more often than not. It was not without reason that she was called 'Lady Hitler'. However, it had been years since she'd felt one of her crisp slaps across her face.

Rhea was standing like a zombie, waiting for the verdict to be pronounced. Meanwhile, Jaspal was trying to pacify Gurleen.

'Go to your room, Rhea. Wait for me there,' Jaspal told her.

Just then, the phone rang and she froze. Mother and daughter both stared at the instrument but neither made an attempt to pick it up. Rhea prayed that it wasn't Rohan. 'Oh, *Babaji*! Please give him enough sense.'

Jaspal finally answered, cutting off the insistent ringing. He listened and then handed it to Rhea. It was Aditi.

'Is anyone on the extension?'

'No.'

'Rohan called me. He thought something was wrong when you abruptly hung up and he wanted me to check on you. Is everything alright?'

'No.'

'Shit! What happened?'

'I'm going to finish the second half of *Twelfth Night* tonight. Then we can do a revision of the entire book tomorrow.'

'Oh, God! Is everyone around you?'

'Yes.'

'Were you caught talking to Rohan? He thinks that might have been the case. He's shitting bricks right now.'

'You're absolutely right. Don't ask. It is very tough. Anyway, you come home tomorrow and we'll study together. I'll call you in the morning.'

She disconnected the call, handed her father the cordless, went to her room and waited.

She sat on her bed, *Twelfth Night* in hand.

If music be the food of love, play on;
Give me excess of it, that, surfeiting,
The appetite may sicken, and so die.
That strain again! It had a dying fall:
O, it came o'er my ear like the sweet sound,
That breathes upon a bank of violets,
Stealing and giving odour! Enough; no more:
'Tis not so sweet now as it was before.
O spirit of love! How quick and fresh art thou,
That, notwithstanding thy capacity
Receiveth as the sea, nought enters there,
Of what validity and pitch soe'er,
But falls into abatement and low price,
Even in a minute: so full of shapes is fancy
That it alone is high fantastical.

Those opening lines of the play, spoken by Duke Orsino, were her favourite and by now she knew them by heart. Just then, Gurleen came in. Rhea sat upright on the bed, surprised. She was expecting her father to come and talk to her. She kept her eyes glued to the book. Words were dancing in front of her.

'Listen carefully to what I have to say. This is not acceptable in our family. Your father told me that this boy is not a Sikh. What are you planning to do? Get married? This is no time to have affairs and that too outside our community. I don't want you meeting him or talking to him now. The entire town has just about stopped talking about your broken engagement. Do you want to give them an opportunity to open their mouths again? If I find out that you're still in touch with this boy, you can forget about going to college in Mumbai. You will not answer any phone calls. If the call is for you, you will be called. No more birthday parties, no more nights out and no more going to the Gymkhana. Is this what you give us in return for the trust we put in you and the freedom we gave you? Consider this my final warning, Rhea.'

Once the monologue stopped, Rhea looked at her mother with tears in her eyes but that didn't have any effect on her.

'Have I made myself clear?'

'Yes.' She was doomed.

'Don't think I'm going to forget about this. And tell that boy I want to meet him tomorrow evening at the club.'

'Mumma, there's no need for that. I won't be in touch with him from now on. I promise.'

'Let me decide whether there is any need for it or not. For now, do as I say.'

She walked out, leaving Rhea emotionally drained and crabby at the same time.

The next day, Aditi came over to meet her in the morning and Rhea told her everything that had happened and the ultimatums that were served to her. 'Lady Hitler wants to meet Rohan. I don't know what's going to happen. You know how her temperament is. What if she's mean and rude to him? I'm so scared.'

Aditi tried to calm her down and said she would speak to Rohan and tell him about it. 'Let's see what he does.'

It turned out that Rohan was actually ballsy enough to meet Gurleen. Rhea later got to know that there was no high drama when the two met. In fact, her mother had let him off with a mere warning. Maybe she hadn't expected him to turn up in the first place.

Life got a little difficult for Rhea from then onwards and she missed Rohan. She was barely able to concentrate on her studies. Their exams were a week away now and there were pages and pages to be studied.

A month after that dramatic episode, she finally met Rohan at Aditi's place when her parents were out. She underwent a barrage of emotions when she saw him; a strange concoction of happiness and sadness. She cried many tears and hugged him while he consoled her. In between kisses, he told her that everything would be okay.

'I should get going now. Thanks, Aditi, you've been an angel!' Rohan said and turned to Rhea. 'I love you and hate to see you cry so promise me that you won't. We need to be careful for a couple of months. Once we're in Mumbai, we won't need to worry about anything.' With that, Rohan left for home and Rhea began dancing with joy.

'You guys are totally made for each other!' said Aditi.

They smiled and then got down to studying. The stress of the impending exams was mounting each day. Their seven papers were stretched over a period of four long weeks. They cursed whoever had set the timetable!

A couple of days after the exams finished, the girls were relaxing at Aditi's place. Finding the time right to have a mushy talk with Rohan, Rhea dialled his home number. Since her mother was still keeping a strict vigil over her, there was no way she could call Rohan from her house unless Gurleen was out.

Rohan's mother informed her that he had gone out and would be home in an hour. Rhea decided to call back later. That day, she called Rohan seven times over five hours before she absolutely had to leave for home. Four were blank calls, during two of which she spoke to his mother. She asked Aditi to make one last desperate call. Rhea went home with a nagging feeling and some unanswered questions in her head. *Where is he? Why isn't he home yet? Who is he with?*

Rhea slept fitfully that night. The next morning, she woke up with a queasy feeling. *Where was Rohan?*

She went looking for her mother and asked if Aditi had called. 'No, she hasn't. You remember *na* we all have to go to Kuldeep Uncle's house for lunch today.'

She had to wriggle out from that. Once her parents were out, she could speak to Rohan in peace for at least an hour.

'Mumma, my stomach is upset and I've had a headache ever since I've woken up. I don't think I can go.'

'Oh! Do you want to take a medicine? And what will you eat? I haven't made anything at home.'

'You can make some *dahi-chawal*. I'm not that hungry anyway.' She couldn't wait for them to leave.

As soon as the house was empty, Rhea grabbed the phone and dialled the all too familiar number. He answered.

'Where were you yesterday? I called so many times. You never even left a message for me with Aditi.'

For the next 10 minutes, Rhea was silent while he spoke. She was shell-shocked at what she was hearing. Was this some kind of a joke? Was he breaking up with her? 'What are you saying, baby? I can't understand where this is coming from. What has happened that you're telling me this all of a sudden?'

'I'm not confident about the kind of marks I'll get and whether they'll be sufficient for me to get admission in a good Mumbai college. I might have to study in another city.'

'You're breaking up with me for that? Can we cross the bridge when we come to it, please? Our results won't be out for another three weeks. Why are you being pessimistic? I'm sure you've done well.'

'No, I haven't, and besides, I don't this see relationship going anywhere. Your parents will never accept me.'

'Where did my parents come into this now? Are you upset about something? I know it hasn't been easy on us ever since my mother found out but things will change when we go to Bombay. You said so yourself a few weeks ago,' wailed Rhea.

For the next 15 minutes, she cried, pleaded, howled, reasoned, fought and shouted. But none of this had any effect on Rohan. His mind seemed to be made up.

Rhea was shattered. Their one-and-a-half year relationship was over just like that. Beyond a point, Rhea saw no more sense in pleading with him. If he didn't want her, he didn't want her. She wouldn't force herself on him. Banging the phone down and telling him to go to hell, she ran to her room, feeling sick to the pit of her stomach. She howled and howled until there were no more tears left to shed.

Rohan's book, *Nothing Lasts Forever*, was still lying unread on her bedside. She picked up the book and hurled it towards the dustbin. 'I hate you! I really hate you! I really do!' Her first love had left her with a shattered heart and a bitter taste in her mouth.

Much later in life, Rhea would find out that Rohan had acted thus on someone's advice. Amit Bhatia, a childhood friend of his who was already studying in Mumbai's Wilson College, had imparted some 'words of wisdom' the day Rhea was frantically trying to call Rohan from Aditi's house.

'Don't carry any extra baggage when you come here to study. It's a whole new world. You know what I mean, right?' Amit had told him and Rohan had listened. Rohan had listened!

7

Old Fish is Goldfish!

Play!
Unbreak my heart!
Say you'll love me again!
Undo this hurt you caused when you walked out the door
And walked out of my life...
Uncry these tears, I cried so many nights!
Unbreak my heart!

'Stop listening to this song! That bastard! How could he do this to you?' Aditi was livid when she found out what Rohan had done.

She immediately called up Jaskaran and, after giving him the lowdown, asked him to speak to Rohan. Rhea snatched the phone from her. 'Jas, I don't want you to speak to him. I will not have anyone begging him to take me back in his life.'

Jaskaran promised her he wouldn't talk to Rohan.

Meanwhile, Aditi was still trying to put a finger on what the real reason might have been for him breaking up. 'There's something fishy here. I can't understand why he did this. He was so in love with you and to suddenly break up just before going to college is...'

Aditi paused to think and then came a varied amount of expressions on her face, ranging from anger to disgust to pure fury and finally, realisation. 'Fucking shit! He is such an asshole. Riu, I can't believe he stooped so low.'

Rhea couldn't understand what was going on in Aditi's mind. 'Please stop building up the suspense. Tell me what you're thinking,' appealed Rhea.

'Forget the crap he told you about his marks and not being sure about getting admission in Bombay. He knows that in whichever city he gets admission, he will be meeting a lot of new people, girls, to be precise. His options open up, don't they? Obviously, he doesn't want to go to college with a girlfriend. The more I think about it, the more certain I am.'

'You think so? Why didn't this strike me? You're probably right. I can't think of any other explanation. I feel like such a fool. Men are such bastards.'

And that was how Rhea's distrust and anger with men began. First it was Happy who had called off their engagement without a word and now, the love of her life, Rohan, had unceremoniously kicked her out of his life without a second thought. Was this how her existence would be?

'Are you listening to me? Where are you lost, Riu? I'm asking you something important,' Aditi was saying.

'Sorry. What did you say?'

'I said, did you guys "do it"?'

'No, Adu! How can you even ask me such a question? If we had, I would have told you. You know I don't believe in pre-marital sex.'

'Thank God! I'm glad you didn't lose your virginity to him. He was totally not worth it.'

'He wasn't a bad guy. He's just...'

'Stop taking his side, Rhea. You're unbelievable! It's over.'

The finality of those words took the wind out of her sails. Rhea had cried so much over the last couple of days that she had absolutely no energy left for the histrionics that came with a broken heart. Only silent tears streamed down her cheeks.

'It's okay, baby! Please don't cry. Think about the brighter side. You can also find someone in Mumbai who will value you for who you are.'

'I'm not interested in anyone.' She sulked.

'You'll change your mind,' Aditi smiled and added, 'Come, let's go to the Gymkhana. They're playing that new Salman Khan movie today, *Pyaar Kiya To Darna Kya*.'

Rhea gave Aditi an 'are-you-kidding-me' look and they both laughed.

'Fate seems to be having a good laugh at my expense! *Nothing Lasts Forever* and *Pyaar Kiya To Darna Kya*! *Pyaar* my foot! Destiny loves to garnish the irony in life with salt and pepper and serve it to me on a platter!' said Rhea, feeling slightly better after venting.

'Oooh! I'm so impressed with your destiny and irony foo-fah! Now go wash your face and get ready,' said Aditi, pushing her towards the bathroom.

Thankfully, Rohan did not turn up at the Gymkhana and the girls were relieved. However, there would be no avoiding him on results day, which was a couple of weeks away. Rhea tried hard not to think about it. There had been absolutely no interaction between them since the break-up.

Moreover, even their group suddenly seemed to have disintegrated. Anuj was busy with Rachel, while Jaskaran and Aditi had stopped talking to Rohan in order to show their solidarity towards Rhea.

On the home front, Jaspal sometimes wondered about the sudden change in Rhea's behaviour. He noticed that she was more subdued and stayed aloof most of the time when she was home. He told himself it was due to jitters about the exam results.

Rhea brooded over her lost love and immersed herself in numerous romance novels. At least in that escapist world, every story had a happy ending. While she put up a brave act in front of Aditi, she cried for Rohan endlessly when she was alone. This was not how first love was supposed to end!

A fortnight later, D-Day had arrived and both Rhea and Aditi were praying for good grades. They were waiting with the rest of their batchmates near St. J's notice board for the results to be pinned up. Rhea was nervous about Rohan's presence on campus. She tried not to look around for him.

Calculators in hand, the girls were beyond themselves by the time the results were out and Rohan was forgotten. Rhea's average was 81.89 per cent, while Aditi's was 78.63 per cent, which, when rounded off, would be 82 and 79 per cent respectively. Mumbai was calling.

1998
Mumbai

Getting admission in St. Xavier's College came with its share of difficulties. Mumbai students got first preference and then there were the high cut-off marks to beat. Even Rhea barely made it in the first list, whereas Aditi had to wait another five days before the second list reluctantly included her name. They were pleased beyond words. With a contact in the Mantralaya through Surinder Uncle's friend, they even got admission in a girls' hostel on Marine Drive. Everything had been set up for them to explore Mumbai and live their lives!

Their Xavier's gang comprised a with-it bunch: Myra, Megha, Ishita, Gaurav and David. Rhea and Aditi got along with them like a house on fire.

Jaskaran, with his 93 per cent score, hadn't been keen on studying in Mumbai. More ambitious than the rest, he chose Delhi's St. Stephen's as his alma mater. Anuj decided to check out colleges in smaller cities like Nagpur and Pune with his measly percentage. As for Rohan, they couldn't care less about him and had no idea where he had ended up.

Aditi was surprisingly mature about Jaskaran's decision to study in Delhi. She seemed not to give much thought to being in a long-distance relationship. Both Rhea and Aditi took to new friends, hostel life, a lively college environment and, most importantly, to freedom, like fish to water. They experienced their first night out on the town, their first visit to a discotheque, the first time they got thoroughly drunk and their first cigarette (which they hated).The girls were living it up!

In the midst of their first semester, Rhea's mother had news for her during one of her weekly calls. When she hung up, she was angry and irritated beyond words. There was apparently a 'boy' they wanted her to meet in Mumbai.

'Please don't do this to me again, Mumma! I'm just in my first year of college. I don't want to meet anyone. Let me finish these three years in peace, please. I'm begging you. I agreed the first time round and look what happened. I am in no hurry to get married. Please understand.' Rhea had disconnected the call.

Then, of course, she felt guilty and called Gurleen back to apologise but stuck to her stand. She couldn't believe this was happening to her again. Why wasn't Rohan with her? She needed to have his strong arms around her and tell her everything would be okay. But who was she kidding? He might already be with another girl by now. *Asshole!* Her thoughts would hover back to him from time to time but the memories hurt less now.

Rhea believed in destiny. If it was meant to be, it would happen. Her belief was fortified when she bumped into him the following week!

Rhea, Aditi and Megha had gone to the Government Law College in Mumbai to meet one of Megha's friends. Just after they entered the premises, Rhea spotted him sitting with a bunch of boys. *Thank God he's not with a girl*, was the first thought that came to her mind.

Aditi spotted him at the same time. 'Don't react, but I've just spotted Rohan. 10 o'clock.'

'I saw. Fuck him,' said Rhea, sticking out her chin.

'He's coming here. Damn!' Aditi panicked on her behalf and Rhea's heart was racing.

'Relax, girls! Let me deal with him,' said Megha, who was fully clued in to both girls' love and life stories.

'Megha, don't say anything. Let's just go,' said Rhea, not wanting to be a part of any nasty conversations.

Too late!

'Hi! I thought from a distance that it was you,' said Rohan, addressing Rhea. 'Hi, Aditi. How are you? It's good to see you both after so long.'

'We're fine and in a hurry. See you around,' said Aditi before Rhea could respond. Aditi and Megha walked ahead and Rhea started to follow. Rohan caught up with her.

'Meet me sometime. I miss you.'

That was rather direct and Rhea was at the risk of melting if this went on for even a minute longer! But she conveyed none of this emotion. 'Go to hell.'

'I made a mistake. Will you give me a chance to explain myself, please? Everyone deserves a second chance. Please meet me later,' begged Rohan.

'Let's go, Rhea.' Aditi and Megha were waiting.

'I need to think. I'll let you know.' She started walking towards her friends and he didn't stop her. The girls were angry with her for having even a small conversation with him.

'Fuck! I'm still in love with him. I am such a fool.' She felt ashamed to admit it.

'Don't get back together with him. I'm sure he wants you to. He must have realised that Bombay girls are not so easy to *patao* and so he wants you back in his life,' Megha said.

'Shouldn't I give him a second chance or maybe just a chance to explain himself?'

'If you really want to, you can hear him out but don't start seeing him again. He'll drop you without thinking twice if someone better comes along.' Megha seemed so much wiser than her.

With that, the topic was closed for discussion and Rhea was left grappling with varied emotions.

Back at the hostel, Aditi brought up the topic when they were alone in their room. 'I know how you feel but don't give in too easily, Riu. Make him wait, otherwise he'll take you for granted.'

The next afternoon, Rhea was reading a book in her room when the hostel guard informed her that she had a visitor. *Who could it be? No one was due to visit her.*

She quickly freshened up, went down and looked around the room. Her eyes moved past him in a hurry and then were back on him again as she realised who her visitor was. Rohan got up as soon as he saw her. 'Hi! I hope I didn't disturb you. You weren't sleeping, were you?'

'I wasn't. What are you doing here?'

'Can we go for a walk?'

'Ummm. Okay.' *Might as well get it over with.*

They walked side by side on Marine Drive. Rhea loved the hustle-bustle of the city.

'How have you been?'

'Good! Alive, as you can very well see.'

'Please don't be sarcastic. I'm trying to mend things.'

'Oh, really. Do I have a say in it this time?'

'Rhea, I'm sorry for hurting you. I really am. I realise how stupid I have been. I've cursed myself all these days. I want to make it up to you and take away all the pain and hurt I've caused you.'

She was silent. Even the noise of the traffic seemed to have stopped all of a sudden, as if wanting to give her some peace and quiet. She looked behind to see cars waiting at the traffic signal. Silence was just what she wanted because if she spoke, she would cry and that was the last thing she wanted to do.

'Say something, baby.'

'DO NOT "baby" me!'

Anger! Yes, that was the correct reaction.

With that little outburst, Rohan gave her the space she wanted and didn't speak. They walked in silence. Soon, they were at the fag end of Nariman Point where the towering NCPA building stood just across the road.

'Do you want to sit here?' asked Rohan.

'Yes.'

Amongst the clamour of vendors, horse carts, evening walkers, lovers and children galore, Rhea and Rohan sat in silence on the steps leading into the Arabian Sea. After some time, he took her hand in his and she let him.

'I'm so sorry, *jaan*. I really am.'

'I hate you.' And the tears that she'd been controlling finally splashed over her cheeks. He hugged her close and she instantly felt at home. She put her arms around him, soaking in his body's warmth and the scent of his D&G! Rhea was so engulfed in her emotions that she almost had a mini-heart attack when Rohan suddenly jumped up.

'Why did you pinch my butt so hard?'

'What? Are you mad? Why would I do that? My hands were around your neck all the time.'

'Then what the hell was that?'

They quickly got up and looked around and saw a baby crab making its way into a stony crevice. Rhea laughed till her stomach hurt. 'Oh my God! A crab has bitten you. Justice has been served.'

'Stop laughing, you mad girl. That really hurt. Stupid crab!'

But Rohan was also laughing by now. Despite all the warnings and words of advice from her friends, she knew in her heart that she was with him from this moment on. He had come back to her. They were meant to be!

8

Love Rollercoaster

Now, college life was a million times more amazing. While the girls were upset with her initially for having given in so easily, they softened up towards him when they realised that Rohan was truly making amends. However, one tiny thing gnawed at Rhea's conscience. 'Should I tell him about it? What if he finds out from someone else?' she asked Aditi.

'You don't owe him any explanation, Riu. You were not in a relationship with Rohan when it happened, so technically you were not cheating on him. It's as simple as that. It was a mistake and it was just one kiss! Besides, how will Rohan ever come to know about it unless one of us tells him? I'm sure Anuj will never utter a word to him about this.'

A few months ago, Jaskaran and Anuj had visited them in Mumbai. In a weak, inebriated moment when they were at a party, Rhea and Anuj had kissed. It was the stupidest thing she'd ever done and it should not have happened. The next day, she was consumed with guilt and blocked the incident from her mind. Both Anuj and Rhea pretended like it had never happened. It was easier that way.

Now that Rhea was back with Rohan, that kiss was weighing on her conscience. Aditi told her to forget about it and she did, until Anuj returned to Mumbai for another visit. She had a feeling of dread in the pit of her stomach but she forced herself to stop thinking about it.

Rhea, Rohan, Aditi, Anuj, Megha, Ishita, Gaurav and David went to a few pubs that night. After the last of the places they went to shut down at 1.30 a.m., they headed to Marine Drive and cosied up at the Marine Plaza coffee shop for the midnight buffet.

'Let's play Truth or Dare!' that was Anuj's bright idea.

The game was fun until it was Rhea's turn to choose and, as luck would have it, it was Anuj who was questioning her. She chose 'truth', afraid that he would give her a horrible task as a dare. But she was aghast at the question he asked her; the only one she didn't want to answer. 'So, Rhea, how many guys have you kissed till date?'

She could have given a tongue-in-cheek reply—baby boys were also categorised as male, right? But she knew what Anuj meant and any smart repartee vanished into thin air because of the guilt she was feeling. 'Why! That's such a silly question! Only one, of course.' She replied confidently and kicked him under the table at the same time.

Everyone knew that Rohan had been the one and only love of her life. There were only two other people on the table who knew about the other guy she had kissed: Aditi and Anuj.

Rhea's heart was pounding and even Aditi was shell-shocked at Anuj's insensitivity. The rest of the night was uneventful and Rhea avoided talking to Anuj altogether. How could he put her in a situation like that? What a complete jerk!

It was almost 5 a.m. and the group was tired but they couldn't go back to their hostels for another hour or so.

Rohan asked Rhea if she wanted to go for a walk. She looked at him, wondering why he wanted to walk at this hour but went along nonetheless. No one else was interested so they bid goodbye to the group and left.

'Some energy you have! My hostel is at the other end of Marine Drive. Are you sure you want to walk so much, baby?' asked Rhea.

'We'll take a cab if you're tired.'

Something was not right. Rhea could feel it in Rohan's tone. Yet, he didn't give anything away. They started walking and after about 10 minutes, Rhea's worst fear came true!

'Is there something you want to tell me?' he asked, wearing a deadpan expression.

'What could I possibly want to tell you?' Rhea tried to appear calm.

'I felt you kicking Anuj under the table when he asked you that question. I'm asking you again. Is there something I should know?'

Fuck! How could she possibly tell him that she had kissed Anuj? There was no way she was going to tell him the truth. 'I kicked him for asking me an idiotic question. There's nothing more to it,' she said, standing her ground.

'You're sure? Anuj told me something else altogether.'

'What are you talking about? What has he told you?'

Unbelievable! Either Rohan was fibbing to extract the truth or he knew! Fuck! He knew! She was so doomed!

'You're sure you don't want to tell me?'

'What's with so many questions? Just tell me what he told you, Rohan!'

'He told me that you guys kissed.'

'What a bastard! It was a mistake.'

'I've known it for some time now. I knew even before I met you at my college.'

'Are you trying to tell me that you're okay with it?'

'How can I be okay with it? I didn't like it at all but I knew I can't hold it against you because we were not together when it happened. But it is bothering me.'

'So what do you want to do? Break up with me again?' *Why did these idiotic tears gather at the drop of a hat?* She was so irritated with herself.

Rhea's hostel was not far away. There were five minutes left before she would be allowed back inside.

'I didn't say I want to break up with you. Seeing Anuj just reminded me of it and it's fucking my mind.'

'It's your call. Decide what you want to do. All I can tell you is that it was a mistake, which happened because we were really drunk. It was just one kiss. Anyway, I have to go now.'

'Alright! Bye!' said Rohan and walked away.

Oh my God! Was he doing it to her again? She had taken a chance and thrown the ball in his court! Had she made a mistake? She couldn't look back now. Forcing herself to walk inside the hostel gates, she held in her tears till she reached her room and had no idea when sleep overtook her.

When she awoke, it was because of a knock on the door. One of the hostel residents was at the door telling her that someone was waiting for her at the bus stop. She looked at the time. It was only 8 a.m. and Aditi was fast asleep on the other bed. It had to be Rohan! She had cried herself to sleep and was a mess. She quickly ran to the balcony of her floor and peered down but a coconut tree hid the bus stop so she couldn't see her visitor.

She had no choice but to go down. She changed her clothes, brushed her teeth and started heading downstairs, when suddenly she remembered something. If it indeed was Rohan waiting outside, then there was something she needed to take care of before going down.

She ran back to her room and took out a Band-Aid from her side table and stuck it on the inside of her left palm. In a fit of anger and love that she had felt towards Rohan, Rhea had taken a safety pin and forcefully scratched 'RS' inside her palm. She was so numb with the way the night had ended that there had been absolutely no pain.

With the scratched wound well hidden, she went to meet her visitor. His back was towards her but she knew it was Rohan. She took a deep breath and walked tentatively towards him. As if on cue, he turned and gave her half a smile. Rhea didn't know what that meant. Did he want her in his life or not?

'I'm sorry I woke you up but I just had to see you. Have you been crying? Look at your eyes!'

'What do you want?'

'I want you.'

'Even after you know that I've kissed Anuj?'

Was this SNAFU situation in her life about to be reversed?

'Yes! I behaved stupidly. It's not like I didn't know about it before. Anuj told me himself a couple of months back when I had gone to Nagpur to meet him. We were stoned and it slipped out of his mouth. Talking about it to you yesterday angered me. I was jealous because I love you a lot and can't bear the thought of you and anyone else.'

'Since when have you started smoking up?'

'It was just that one time. Ummm, okay! Don't give me that look. I've smoked up a couple of times but I don't like it so I'm not going to do it again. Anyway, we're digressing from the topic.'

'And what exactly is the topic?'

'I love you, baby, and I'm sorry for the way I behaved yesterday. I don't want to lose you again. I really don't.'

He took her hands in his and pulled her closer. Rhea winced as his fingers pressed against her palm. He noticed her expression and her hand. 'What is this? It wasn't there yesterday or even this morning.'

He began removing the Band-Aid and she quickly pulled her hand away. 'It's nothing. Just a scratch.'

Rohan wasn't convinced. 'Did you hurt yourself? Let me see.'

Rhea knew he wouldn't rest until he found out what had happened. She was suddenly feeling shy and stupid for having done what she did. Rohan was carefully peeling off the tape from her hand and was shocked at what he saw. 'My God! What have you done to yourself, you stupid girl? You've got my initials on your palm? You're unbelievable.'

He hugged her to him but not before she noticed a thin film of tears in his eyes. 'Don't ever hurt yourself for me again. Do you understand? Oh! I am such a fool!'

Rhea nodded, acknowledging both his statements, and smiled against his chest. 'I love you and I'm sorry for whatever happened with Anuj.'

'Forget about it. It doesn't matter. I think I should let you get back to your beauty sleep. Call me on the hostel number when you wake up and we'll go out for dinner in the evening.'

'Okay! You too get some rest.'

He kissed her on her forehead and bid her goodbye. Rhea was happy again.

Over the next few months, another relationship was under scrutiny when Aditi and Jaskaran decided to break up. After almost a year of being in a long-distance relationship, they admitted to each other that it wasn't working. They had one of the most amiable break-ups ever.

Time was flying and before they knew it, they were in the final year of college. Everyone was discussing his or her next move. Rhea would remain unnaturally quiet at these discussions. Gurleen was only thinking about her marriage and constantly told her so. Rhea had no idea what she wanted to do. She had no idea if her parents would want her to come back to Jalandhar after college. She didn't know if she could convince them to let her stay on in Mumbai. She needed to get out of her torpor and decide the next course of action, pronto.

All her friends were planning to do a diploma course in advertising and marketing. For the time being, she too hopped on the bandwagon and filled up relevant admission forms for various institutions.

Two months before their final year exams were due, Rohan's mother fell seriously ill in Jalandhar and he was called home. Given the situation, he wasn't sure whether he would be able to give his exam. Rhea was devastated but she had to concentrate on the exams. She stayed strong and refused to be swept away in the tide of her own emotions.

This too shall pass.

Eventually, Rohan wrote his exam via correspondence. It was doubtful that he would ever return to Mumbai. His mother was recovering well but his family wanted him to join his father's law firm, Shroff & Associates Pvt. Ltd., and settle down in Jalandhar.

Rhea also went home after her exams with the motive of convincing her parents to let her pursue a diploma course from Xavier Institute of Communications, where she had already applied for admission. She was also hoping she could spend some time with Rohan.

Convincing her father to let her study more wasn't too difficult and he in turn convinced Gurleen after a few discussions. That part of her life seemed temporarily sorted, but things with Rohan were not going too well. He seemed to have retreated into a shell since returning to Jalandhar. It had been almost 10 days since Rhea had been home but she hadn't seen him yet.

One day while talking to him on the phone, Rhea lightly mentioned that he hadn't made any effort to meet her and that she missed him. The fiery words that came out of his mouth in reply stunned Rhea into silence. He began shouting at the top of his voice. 'You are a bloody selfish bitch. Do you know that? You're only concerned about your own feelings. I don't even know why we're still in this relationship. You just don't understand the situation that I am in. Do you? Go to hell, Rhea, and don't call me up again. I don't ever want to see your face.'

Rhea was so hurt by his words that she started shivering from head to toe. She ran to her room and began crying inconsolably. What had gotten into him? How could he be so downright rude? 'I hate my life. I hate Rohan. Mumma will never agree to our relationship and what is the point anyway when he also hates me and doesn't want to see my face ever? It's best to end my life! I don't want to live anymore.' Rhea mumbled in between her tears and locked her room.

She found some strips of medicines in the bedside table that her grandmother had left behind during her last visit. She consumed them all without giving a thought to the consequences.

She lay down on her bed and waited for it to engulf her. She felt drowsy but saw none of the white light that she had read about in books. Her pain and hurt were now fading. She had no regrets in ending her life. What was life without Rohan, anyway?

And then there was blissful peace! It didn't hurt anymore.

Rhea woke up feeling very weak and confused. Her mother was crying, sitting next to her. She was in a room that she didn't recognise. As consciousness slowly crept in, her fuzzy brain remembered what she had done.

'Rheaaaa! What would we have done if we had lost you?'

Hearing Gurleen's pained voice, Rhea felt immense remorse. Why was she always the one making her mother cry? She had been so engulfed in the pain caused by Rohan's words that she hadn't stopped to think twice about the effect her actions would have on her family.

They all surrounded her now, in a room, which she figured was in a hospital. All of Jalandhar would come to know that she had tried to commit suicide. The enormity of the situation hit her suddenly and she cried for what her parents might have faced because of her.

She wanted some time alone with her father. Jaspal understood without her having to voice this wish. He asked everyone to wait outside.

'Why did you do this, Rhea? I wasn't even aware that you were unhappy about something. You should have spoken to me. We have been so worried. We would never be able to forgive ourselves if something had happened to you. What is bothering you so much? Do you want to talk about it?'

'Papa, I'm really sorry about what I did. It was so stupid of me. Rohan was very angry with me for no reason and he said some very mean things to me. I was very upset. Don't tell Mumma about Rohan. We will have to tell her something else. How long have I been here? Does Rohan know about this? He can't know.'

'You don't worry about Mumma or Rohan right now. I will think of something to tell her. Try to get some sleep now. The doctor should be coming to see you any moment now.'

The news about Rhea's hospital stint spread far and wide amongst family and friends in Jalandhar and elsewhere. She got calls from so many of her relatives who wanted to know what had happened and if she was okay. Rhea was ashamed. She had no right to take her own life. The official story was that she had taken some wrong medicines by mistake and those had caused a serious allergic reaction. Of course, there were other whispers doing the rounds but no one wanted to ask her family to confirm them.

Rohan heard about the incident too and had frantically tried to reach her over the phone everyday. She refused to speak to him. He was bold enough to even come to her house once but Gurleen wouldn't let him meet her.

Rhea loved him a lot but didn't want to meet him. She wanted to see how life would be without him. She had to test herself because she would never be so weak again.

People said that absence made the heart grow fonder. In her case, she hoped that out of sight would soon become out of mind.

'I Will Survive' became her favourite song.

Play!
At first I was afraid, I was petrified,
Kept thinking I could never live without you by my side,
But then I spent so many nights thinking how you did me wrong,
And I grew strong, and I learned how to get along!

Rhea was due to leave for Mumbai soon to begin her course in advertising and marketing from XIC. She was tired of the heartbreaks and wanted to be free from all emotional entanglements.

After what she'd done, she had to try a lot harder to convince her parents to let her go. She was ever so grateful to her father for his unrelenting support. Rhea promised him that she would never harm herself again and it was a promise she meant to keep.

Once she was back in Bombay, Rohan's attempts to get back in touch with her increased. He paged and emailed her everyday. She refused to read any of the messages. When she acquired her first mobile phone, he got hold of her number within a few weeks. He sent her a text message one day, full of guilt and regret about how he had spoken to her in anger that fateful day.

Rhea had ignored him for a long time now and her heart was at the risk of forgiving him yet again. Before the battle between her heart and mind began in full earnest yet again, Rhea replied back to his message with a curt, 'It's okay.'

That was all it took. A full-fledged conversation ensued between them thereafter and neither could deny what they felt for the other.

By now, Rhea, Aditi, Ishita and Megha were staying together in an apartment they had taken up in Bandra. The girls thoroughly disapproved of Rhea's decision to get back with Rohan after what had happened, particularly because they believed long-distance relationships hardly worked. However, she was blind when it came to Rohan and chose to turn a deaf ear to them.

Now that there were no hostel restrictions, the girls went out more often. This sometimes didn't go down well with Rohan, who had started working at his father's firm in Jalandhar. He would occasionally show signs of jealousy but was always careful with his words. Rhea could sense his insecurity. He didn't tell her in so many words but when he asked pointed questions about her male friends, she sometimes wondered if he suspected her of having an affair.

Rhea began to feel as if something was amiss. Slowly but surely, she knew that her heart was no longer in this relationship like before. Soon enough, her mother began coaxing her again to consider boys for marriage. The mobile phone suddenly morphed into a bane rather than a boon.

She decided to come clean with Rohan and poured her heart out to him. She was falling out of love. Long distance was not working for her. Her parents were looking out for prospective boys for her and would never agree to their marriage. They had no future together. Of course she loved him. He would always be special to her but she wasn't 'in love' with him anymore.

Rohan hadn't seen this coming. He was taken aback. How could she do this to him? Rhea was angry at his accusation. He could do the same to her, not once but twice, and she was the villain if she voiced her feelings? However, Rhea wasn't thinking on 'tit for tat' terms. Their relationship was just not working for her. She wanted to end things cordially but more often than not, a break-up was anything but that.

They were both angry and didn't speak to each other for a couple of weeks.

Rhea's birthday was around the corner and all she wanted to do was let her hair down and not think. On the day, she was finalising plans for the evening with her friends when the doorbell rang! She opened the door and was aghast to find Rohan at the door with a huge bouquet of red roses.

'What are you doing here?'

'What kind of a welcome is that? Happy birthday, Rhea!' He was hurt by her reaction but tried not to show it.

'I'm sorry and thank you. Why don't you come in?'

The girls were shocked to see him. They wondered what would happen at the party they had organised for the night. Their other friends were due to join them and Rohan didn't know any one. After everything that Rhea had gone through in the last month or so, they didn't want anything to spoil her birthday. But the damage was already done!

Rhea behaved standoffishly with Rohan. She didn't have anything to say to him and he looked out of place in their apartment.

'I thought you would be happy to see me here and that's the reason I decided to surprise you but clearly I was wrong. I think it's best if I go. You have a good birthday. I'm leaving tomorrow night. It would be nice if we could meet before that. I'm staying with Rohit, remember him from school? I'll message you his number.'

'I remember Rohit but I don't see the point of meeting you again. I told you I don't want to be in this relationship anymore.'

'As you wish, Rhea. I'll send you Rohit's number just in case you change your mind. Have a good birthday.'

That night, Rhea got drunk like never before. She had the worst birthday ever and cried her heart out. She felt like a mean bitch for breaking his heart. But she had no choice. They had no future and she had fallen out of love. Her first love was over, and this time it was for good.

Rhea surfaced by early evening the next day with a massive hangover. A few cups of coffee and lots of water later, she felt better.

'Oh shit! Rohan! What time did he say his train was?' The caffeine had kick-started Rhea's system. It was almost 6 p.m. She had slept through the day! She checked her phone but there were no missed calls.

Rohit! Call up Rohit! Rohan had sent her his number last night. She dialled it. *Pick up! Pick up! Pick up!*

After what seemed like an eternity, Rohit answered. 'Hi Rhea!'

'Hi, Rohit! Is he around? May I please speak to him?'

Rohit's 'knight in shining armour' dialogue from Shaila's birthday party long ago suddenly popped into her mind. She swooshed it aside.

'I've come to drop him to the station. He's heading back to Jalandhar. The train is leaving in five minutes.'

'Please can you give him the phone? It's really important. Rohit, I need to say bye to him. Make me speak to him. Please.'

'Hold on!'

'Rohan! Is that you? Say something. Please. I'm sorry about whatever happened.'

'Bye, Rhea. I understand your decision. You'll always be special to me. Have a good life.'

He disconnected the line and just like that, her now-on-now-off first love of almost six years was over. *Finito!*

9

Arranged Marriage

2003
Mumbai

'I think Gaurav likes you. Have you seen the way he looks at you? He's like a doting puppy,' Aditi told Rhea.

'My days of puppy love are over, Adu! I'm not interested in anyone right now. Can I just enjoy being single for a change? Besides, you know Gaurav is not my type.'

Before Aditi could pursue the conversation further, Rhea's phone started ringing. It was her mother, who wasn't quite as Hitler-like as before. She had finally found the courage to open up to her about Rohan and how they had ended their relationship. However, Rhea had made sure to confide in Jaspal before telling Gurleen.

While Rhea still couldn't discuss alcohol and parties with her mother, she could talk to her about the affairs of the heart. The bond between them had become stronger since her lame attempt at ending her life.

'Hi, Mumma! What's happening?'

'Hi, *beta*! Everything's fine here. I hope you are taking good care of yourself.'

After a few minutes spent catching up, Gurleen came to the point.

'Mumaaaaa! Pleaseeee. I don't want to meet any boy.'

'What kind of behaviour is this, Rhea? Just meet him. *Tennu ki farak painda*? No one is asking you to say "Yes" right away.'

Like it had always been, Rhea knew there was no running away from this. She reminded herself she should be glad that her mother didn't make a huge fuss because she had stayed in Mumbai an extra year after college.

'Okay, fine! Send me his details.'

'I'll ask Preet to email the details to you. Just don't be so closed towards marriage.'

'Okay, Mumma! Whatever you say!'

Rhea apprised Aditi of the latest development in her life. Aditi asked her not to worry. 'No one can force you against your will. You're not 15 anymore.'

A day later, an email was waiting for her with a photograph and more details about the boy, Puneet Sodhi, who had been born and brought up in the US. What Rhea found odd was his email ID: manofpuneet@hotmail.com.

Man of Puneet? What the hell was that supposed to mean? She tried not to think too much about it.

He was three years older than her and had just received his medical degree. Currently, he was doing his residency at a hospital in Denver, Colorado.

'Man of Puneet' popped into her head again. But it would be petty of her if she judged him by his email address, right?

He was visiting Mumbai in a week's time with his mother to 'see girls eligible for marriage'. Their mothers had spoken to each other and matched their horoscopes. Let the ordeal begin!

A day before she was due to meet the boy and his mother, Jaspal and Gurleen flew down to Mumbai. A sense of *déjà vu* loomed large over Rhea. She couldn't let history repeat itself. She didn't want to get married right now and she was going to reject this proposal. She was definitely smarter and more mature at 23 than she had been at 15; at least, she hoped she was.

Much to her disappointment, Gurleen had not changed when it came to the subject of finding a husband for her daughter. 'Do you have something yellow to wear? Bittu Maharaj, our *panditji*, has told us that it's an auspicious colour to wear for this meeting. Things will definitely work out. Also, if the boy asks, say you are willing to settle in the US.'

Rhea rolled her eyes. Yellow!

Play!
Look at the stars,
Look how they shine for you
And everything you do
Yeah, they were all yellow!
Pause!

She had recently heard this song by Coldplay and had fallen in love with it. Alas! The stars were not yet shining for her but yellow was! Her mind stopped singing when she realised that Gurleen was waiting for an answer.

'No, Mumma! I don't have anything yellow to wear.'

'Let's go buy something for you right now. We still have a couple of hours before the market shuts.'

Play!
I drew a line,
I drew a line for you,
Oh what a thing to do,
And it was all Yellow.
Pause!

A yellow *salwar kameez* this time round as opposed to a green one last time! *Alright, Bittu Maharaj, I'm putting your predictions to test.* As far as she was concerned, pandits like him were just there to loot people and fuel superstition.

One yellow *salwar kameez* later, they headed back to her uncle's place, where her parents were staying. According to Mr. Bittu, they should meet the boy at 4.45 p.m., which was when the stars were aligned favourably and all that jazz!

Oh yes! The stars…

Play!
Look at the stars,
Look how they shine for you…
Stop! Stop! Stop!

Gurleen was fussing obsessively about being at the meeting place at 4.45 p.m. Rhea tried to dress up and look presentable.

'Put some powder on your face. You've tanned so much recently.' She heard her mother say.

'Powder? Sure, Mumma, if you want me to look like a ghost and scare him away, I will put some on my face right away. I'm not tanned; this is what they call a wheatish complexion.'

Gurleen glared at her but handed her a compact powder kit nonetheless. 'Dab some of this on your face and under the eyes.' This mother was subtly forceful, and how.

Rhea glared back at her but knew better than to argue.

When they finally managed to reach the meeting place, it was at the desired time. Jaspal saw Puneet and his mother, Deeya, at the far end of the restaurant.

'Man of Puneet' got up from the sofa as soon as he saw them approach. Basic etiquette in a man was a big turn-on for Rhea. He was a looker too. The photographs she'd seen of him didn't do any justice to the person standing in front of her.

She berated herself for giving him brownie points on such criteria. That was not part of the plan. She was here to send his 'Indian bride' dreams to the doghouse!

Rhea gave herself a mental shake. Oh! She had a question or two for him and she mentally rubbed her hands in glee just thinking about it.

Play!
Born in the USA!
I was born in the USA!
Stopppp!

Concentrate, you idiot! Rhea was aghast at how songs were popping into her head. That was nothing new but this was not the time.

They joined them at the table and a basic round of introductions took place. Rhea knew that very soon one of the elders would ask her and Puneet to find another table so they could talk in 'private'.

Privacy in a noisy restaurant in the middle of the afternoon with parents sitting a few feet away! What a warped concept!

Fifteen minutes later, his mother had bombarded her with questions galore and extracted as many answers as possible. It was an interview for the position of daughter-in-law, a thorough and unrelenting one at that.

What do you do? What are your plans once you finish your advertising and marketing course? Will you be taking up a job or would you prefer to go back home? Are you open to working after marriage or do you want to be a housewife? How would you like living in the US? Do you know how to cook? Are you religious? Do you pray? Do you know how to drive?

Rhea's head was reeling. She was unprepared for this blitzkrieg. How did anyone prepare for this? Was there some sort of syllabus to refer to? How did it matter if she prayed or not? Did it make her less of a good person if she didn't?

Jaspal was quick to notice that Rhea was ill at ease.

'Puneet, why don't you and Rhea take another table and get to know each other while we wait here?'

'Yeah! Sure, Uncle. That would be very nice.' Puneet said with a thick American accent.

Rhea got up from the table, overtly conscious of her yellow outfit. She was sure she looked like a court jester. She wished she'd worn jeans with a yellow T-shirt instead.

'He's come to India in search of an Indian bride. You can't wear jeans and a T-shirt, Rhea,' Gurleen had said the day before.

Anyway, here she was, seated across from him at another table.

'Sorry about all those questions. Mom can get obnoxious and nosy sometimes and doesn't know when to stop. But I can assure you she didn't mean to intimidate you.'

'Oh! You have nothing to be sorry about. I wasn't intimidated, just caught off guard. I can understand that she would want to know things about me.'

'I think she asked you everything possible! Why don't you ask me anything that you might want to know?'

'Well, I've wondered why you've come to India looking for a bride considering you're born and brought up in the US. Why not look for an Indian girl there? It makes more sense, don't you think?'

Gotcha! She got her desired reaction. He had not seen this coming and it got him thinking! What was the right answer, anyway?

'Wow! Yeah! I know what you mean. Well, I'm 26 years old and my parents want me to get married. They thought it was best if we came to India since we know a lot of people here. And despite being born in the US, I think my brother and I have been brought up with the same Indian values as you.'

'I'm not doubting your values. I'm just saying there's a difference in outlook.'

'Yeah! I guess you're right. Speaking of difference in outlook, do you know of good places to party in Mumbai? My cousins are not allowed to go to clubs and discos and I want to check out the nightlife here. I've heard so much about it from my Indian friends.'

Rhea knew Gurleen would hit the roof if she heard him say this. Trying not to think about her mother's reaction, Rhea obliged nonetheless. 'Well, let's see, there's Enigma, Fire 'N Ice, Velocity, Copa Cabana, Insomnia, Ghetto, Athena, J49, Mikano, Jolly Rogers and Earthquake.' She rattled away, wanting to add, *take your pick.*

'Wow! I should probably write those names down. Do you think you can show me around these clubs sometime?'

Was he serious?

'Well! I'm not too sure about that. My parents are in town this week and also I don't think they would approve.'

Puneet realised his faux pas but it was too late. 'Oh! Of course I understand. I guess I didn't think before asking. Don't take it the wrong way.'

'Not at all. Don't worry about it. If there's anything else that you need to ask me, please feel free.'

As they headed back to the other table, Rhea wasn't sure what to make of him and was surprised when, within five minutes, Jaspal decided to take their leave. Had something happened in her absence?

'Stupid, confused people! Do they even know what they are saying?' Jaspal was fuming as soon as they were out of earshot.

'What happened, Papa? Did his mother say something?'

'Something doesn't even begin to define what she proposed! She wanted you to come to the US and stay with them for a month to see if you adjust well to the family and the place.'

'After the engagement?' Rhea asked tentatively.

'No! No engagement. Without any formal ritual, nothing! Just for a holiday. Can you believe it? I'll be damned if I agreed!'

'She wants me to travel to an unknown country, stay with unknown people and *then* let her decide if she wants me as her daughter-in-law?!'

Rhea then recounted her conversation with Puneet, which made Gurleen even more livid. She was happy she didn't have to make any life-altering decisions.

Rhea wondered what Bittu Maharaj would have to say about this! Whatever happened to wearing the auspicious yellow and scheduling the meeting for 4.45 p.m? She was tempted to ask Gurleen but knew it would only infuriate her further.

For now, she was glad to put it behind her. However, her relief was short-lived. The next morning, a distant relative came to meet her parents and before she knew it, there was another marriage proposal in the offing. What was worse, this new 'candidate' lived very close to where they were staying and could meet them in a few hours.

Damn! Just my luck!

She was grateful that the boy was coming to meet them at Surinder Uncle's place and they wouldn't have to go out anywhere for 'privacy.' After the doctor debacle, this boy was a Chartered Accountant working with Standard Chartered Bank.

'Fine! Bring it on! Let's see what you got in store for me now,' Rhea challenged the universe.

She decided to wear jeans and had a ready retort on the tip of her tongue in case her mother gave her any of the 'Bittu' spiel! Thankfully, she was spared.

Amar Virdhi came to meet her with his parents. The fact that the meeting was at her uncle's home gave Rhea some comfort. She was in her own territory and that increased her confidence.

Sitting in her uncle's room with him for their 'private' talk, Rhea found Amar to be a fun guy. He had a great sense of humour and could well have been one of her friends from college. He loved travelling. He wasn't expecting his wife to be a 'typical' Indian housewife. It seemed perfect.

After discussing their likes and dislikes, their taste in movies and music and their favourite cuisine among other things, Rhea and Amar came out of the room beaming almost an hour and a half later. They had had a great conversation and also exchanged numbers. The families promised to get back to each other.

'How was it? You both spent so much time together and you look so happy!' Gurleen began her inquest.

'He seems like a nice guy and our thoughts are similar on a number of things.'

'Oh! *Wadiya hai ji*! Then we can take this forward.'

Hardly had he left from her uncle's place when he sent Rhea a text message telling her how much he had enjoyed their meeting.

'We must meet for lunch or dinner one of these days,' Amar suggested. Rhea agreed.

Three days later, Rhea was waiting for Amar to pick her up for their first dinner date. He arrived right on time, which impressed her. They had not decided where they were going and as soon as she got inside the car, he handed her a bunch of pink carnations and asked her where she would like to dine. 'Is there a place or cuisine you have in mind?'

A bit surprised with the flowers, Rhea took them and said, 'They're beautiful. Thank you so much. Actually, I was thinking we could go for some Chinese. Mainland China is just around the corner. If you don't mind.'

Mainland China it was and as they reached the entrance, Rhea's faith was reinstated in the fact that chivalry was not dead. Amar held the door for her and she gracefully stepped inside with a smile. When they were seated at their table, Amar let her do the ordering for the starters and main course, while he ordered a single malt for himself and a white wine for Rhea.

By the end of their meal, while Rhea was finishing her second glass of wine, Amar was on his sixth Glenfiddich on the rocks!

'You have amazing capacity, Amar. I'm feeling a buzz with just two glasses and you look sober even after six,' joked Rhea.

'Have you been counting?' He looked serious and Rhea felt embarrassed at what she'd said.

'I'm really sorry if I've offended you. I didn't mean to sound judgmental.' She rebuked herself.

Amar broke into a laugh, which left Rhea confused. 'Relax, I was just joking. You look like someone has died.'

Rhea heaved a sigh of relief. 'You got me. I was scared I'd offended you. And anyway I shouldn't have made that comment.'

'Don't worry about it. I didn't mind.'

Amar refused to let her pay for the bill and insisted on paying. He was quickly ticking off everything on 'The Perfect Guy' list.

Rhea thanked him for a wonderful evening when he dropped her back home. The very next morning, Amar sent her a text message, thus ignoring the three-day rule. 'I had such a great time with you last night. We must do this again.'

And they did meet again...a week later. Amar was a huge Shah Rukh Khan fan so they decided to go for the newly released SRK–Rani Mukerji starrer *Chalte Chalte*. Halfway into the movie, Rhea wasn't sure whether the choice had been a good one. It was all about fights, suspicion and insecurity between two people who had fallen in love and gotten married. Amar was way too involved in the movie but Rhea had lost interest in the marital discord saga after a while. Those two hours 50 minutes seemed never-ending for her as she patiently sat through the entire movie.

'What a brilliant movie! The tagline is so true! Opposites attract! Didn't you just love it?'

Amar's enthusiasm was infectious and Rhea fell in step with him. 'Yes, it was nice.' That was about the only lie she could spout so she didn't burst his bubble.

Rhea and Amar started meeting regularly after their second date. She enjoyed his company and he was always attentive towards her. If there was one thing that nagged her, it was his excessive drinking. Not that she was against the idea of him drinking, but it seemed that he drank way more than what was good for him and didn't know when to stop. However, she chose to reserve her comments on that topic for the time being.

A month after Amar and Rhea began dating, Gurleen finally asked her in all seriousness. 'What have you both decided, *beta*? How many more days do you both need? You're mostly alone with him and before people start talking rubbish, you should decide what you want to do. At least let's do a *roka*.'

Rhea had been trying to fend off Gurleen on this topic for some days now. She needed to talk to Amar. He was coming over to her place that evening and she decided that's when she would broach the topic. After a couple of drinks, she told him about her conversation with Gurleen.

'It's a good idea,' said Amar and she was stupefied into silence. When she failed to elicit a response, he stunned her even further by going down on his knees, holding out the bottle opener in his hands as a substitute for a ring.

'Will you marry me?'

'Yes.'

He pretended to put the faux ring on her finger as they came closer to kiss each other.

The mother will be so happy, Rhea thought as she rested her head on his shoulder, while he sipped on his drink.

10

Catastrophe

A day after Rhea informed her mother about their decision, Gurleen and Jaspal had taken a flight from Jalandhar to Mumbai. The *roka* ceremony was held two days later at Surinder Uncle's house. As part of the ritual, he presented Rhea with a beautiful *nath*, which she would be wearing on the day of her wedding. The party began in earnest soon after close family and friends blessed Rhea and Amar and wished them a happy life ahead.

'No courtship period this time round. *Chat mangni, pat byah*! The faster we get them married, the better it will be. It also gives people less time to find flaws when there are none.' Based on her worldly experience, Gurleen had thoroughly thought things through.

The marriage date was set for a month later. Things were on a roll from then on. Before she knew what hit her, Rhea was being draped in beautiful saris, made to try on different pieces of jewellery and continually choosing vibrant *salwar kameezes* for her trousseau. Things were moving very fast but when it seemed right, it seemed right.

Shopping for her trousseau consumed the better part of her days now. To organise and pack the myriad clothes, jewellery, bed sheets and cutlery that had piled up in every nook and corner of her small house was a formidable task in itself.

While all her friends were excited about the wedding, they were also a bit surprised that Rhea was getting married in such haste.

Ten days before the wedding, the rituals began with the *mangni*, where Amar and Rhea formally exchanged rings. Soon after the *mangni*, Amar's mother Pushpinder, did the *sagan* by feeding Rhea boiled rice and milk as was the custom.

'This is all so overwhelming. Tomorrow is the *sangeet* and then *mehndi*. I think by the time the wedding date arrives, I will be a zombie,' Rhea told Aditi when they were alone.

'It'll be over before you know it and then you can relax all you want on your honeymoon. For the time being all you have to do is sit pretty and exude all the newlywed radiance of a blushing bride,' said Aditi dramatically. But before Rhea could retort, Aditi was called away by Jaspal for some work.

Her friend was right. The next few days just flew by. On the day of her wedding, as Rhea stood outside the Andheri Gurudwara in her red *salwar kameez* and her beautiful *chuda*—a combination of red and cream ivory bangles—she was beaming with joy.

Punjabi weddings are synonymous with splendour, magnificence and all things large! True to tradition, Jaspal had left no stone unturned for his daughter's. Rhea had never seen her parents happier and was glad that in a way, she was responsible for bringing them joy.

As Rhea solemnly walked towards the Gurudwara, she saw her 'happily ever after'. The families greeted each other and performed the *ardas*. The *milni* ceremony that followed, where both family members exchanged garlands and greetings, was short and sweet.

Once these rituals were over, Rhea was asked to enter the hall and pay her respects to the Guru Granth Sahib. She saw Amar then, looking resplendent in his wedding finery. Her heartbeat increased as she stepped inside to the soothing and magical sounds of the *kirtan* being sung. As their eyes met, she smiled shyly at him. The *granthi* then began the formal proceedings of the marriage. They were told about the significance of marriage, their duties and obligations towards each other as equal partners in the journey of life.

Amar and Rhea walked around the Guru Granth Sahib four times as directed by the *granthi*. The final *ardas* formally concluded their wedding. They were now husband and wife. Congratulatory messages, hugs, kisses and happiness followed. Lunch at the Gurudwara was finger-licking yummy and although Rhea was bogged down after the ceremony, she was ravenous.

Rhea was stepping contentedly into a new life and that was how she wanted life to be: full of small joys. Almost five hours after she had stepped into the Gurudwara, she bid a tearful adieu to her family and friends. Amar and Rhea were now headed towards the Renaissance Hotel in Powai for the night.

Hardly had they sat in the car that Amar took out a flask from his pocket and took a long, hard swig. She looked at him and laughed.

'That bad, hmmmm! Can't you wait to reach the hotel?'

'It was intimidating, to say the least. I need my alcohol.'

'Don't tell me you were carrying the flask in the Gurudwara. You're unbelievable.'

He smirked and, after emptying the flask, bent and took out a bottle from under the front seat.

'Don't you think you're drinking a lot? Take it easy. You'll be drunk by the time we reach the hotel.'

'Wow! My wife of five minutes has already started nagging me. You know my capacity, so why are you worrying?'

'Why are you talking to me like this? I'm not nagging you.' Rhea was hurt by his words but put it down to wedding jitters.

'Here, have a swig. You'll feel better.'

Rhea declined, saying, 'If I have neat whiskey right now, I'm going to be sick. Maybe I can have a drink at the hotel a little later.'

'Single malt is not whiskey,' Amar corrected her.

Whatever! She didn't like where this was going and decided to let him be.

There was no further conversation between them until they reached their hotel. Rhea made a drink for herself as soon as they checked into their room. She took her glass to the bathroom and decided to soak herself in hot water. The last one month had taken a toll on her. She was tired to the bone.

Eyes shut, glass in hand, Rhea was enjoying some alone time going over the events of the day, when she heard Amar coming inside the bathroom.

Damn! I forgot to lock the door!

While she was suddenly overtly conscious of her nakedness, she refused to open her eyes and decided to ignore him.

'I'm sorry. I know I was rude to you in the car. I just wanted to drink a few sips to calm my nerves. I had been so tense the entire day.'

He surprised her with his apology and she smiled, forgiving him instantly.

'Do you mind if I join you? The bathtub looks really inviting, especially with you inside it.'

Her heart fluttered. They had not had sex while they were dating, Rhea being quite firm on the subject. 'You're quite traditional that way,' Amar had told her, and laughed.

Their bathtub romp involved Amar getting high on alcohol and Rhea on passion.

'I think we should stop drinking now. The hangover is going to kill us tomorrow,' said Rhea after their second round of lovemaking. Her hands had become wrinkly as a result of being in water for more than an hour and she moved to step out. Amar, who was still nursing his drink, stopped her.

'Not yet.'

'Amar, I'm really tired now. I just want to lie down.'

'I *said* not yet.'

'You've had way too much to drink and...'

'I said not yet, didn't I? Sit down.'

This time there was a sharp edge in his voice and Rhea sat down and he leaned forward to engulf her in his arms.

'I don't like the way you're talking to me, Amar.'

'And I don't like it when you don't listen to me.'

Had she made a mistake? Who was this guy?

When Rhea opened her eyes the next morning, she was hurting all over and had a pulsating headache. She saw Amar sleeping next to her on the bed and felt as if she had married a stranger. Rhea's first night of marriage had been memorable but not in a good way. She wasn't going to forget how Amar had forced himself on her twice even when she had protested. The torture had stopped only when he passed out, drunk.

'Good morning.' He was awake, putting a spanner in her thoughts as he stretched his hand towards her waist.

Rhea muttered a quick good morning and hastily went towards the bathroom. This time, she remembered to lock the door.

Rhea wanted to call up Aditi but while Amar was around, there was no way she could speak to anyone about her miserable night. A feeling of dread enveloped her and tears threatened to fall.

'Hey, honey! Are you going to take long in there? I need to use the loo.'

Rhea's eyes widened. He was behaving as if nothing had happened. *Maybe he didn't remember. Maybe he was just pretending not to remember.* She was so lost in her thoughts that she forgot to reply.

'Rhea, are you okay?' He asked.

'Yes. I'll be out in a minute.'

They were due to check out of the hotel by noon. All she wanted was to be in familiar surroundings around people. She took a shower in record time. Draping herself in the large hotel towel, she tentatively stepped into the room.

Amar got up from the bed to give her a hug. 'Good morning, wifey. I'll get ready and then we can head back home.'

He had acted so different last night, cold and rude, and yet here he was this morning, chirpy and behaving as if nothing had happened.

Rhea got dressed and decided to talk to him about his behaviour later in the day. As they walked towards the portico after checking out of the hotel, Amar put his hands around her shoulder and planted a kiss her on her cheeks. The smile on his face seemed genuine.

That entire day, Amar was extra attentive towards her and her needs. The moment they reached his house, he tried to make her comfortable. His parents, who lived two blocks away, were due to come over in an hour.

Do you want some coffee? Are you hungry? Want to order in? Do you want to rest for sometime? Is there anything I can get you?

How he slipped into this caring role so effortlessly after behaving like a monster last night was beyond Rhea's understanding.

Maybe he's feeling guilty about what he did and is ashamed to talk about it. Maybe this is his way of saying sorry. Maybe I'm thinking too much about it and giving it unnecessary importance in my head.

Rhea would realise soon that all she was doing was making excuses for him.

Over the next few weeks, Amar's behaviour became predictable. When he drank himself into oblivion, he would say extremely corrosive and condescending things to her. But the next day, he would transform into a sensitive and caring guy, preparing breakfast and bringing her flowers.

Rhea was slowly getting weary of the bottle in his hand. It had been a month and a half since their marriage and she had not found the courage to speak to anyone about Amar's problem. She kept hoping and thinking that he would change. But it was not to be. She had realised that he was a prisoner to his addiction and would probably stop only when the wheels fell off.

The situation augmented when one day Rhea told him that she was planning to visit her parents in Jalandhar for a week as her XIC classes were getting over. Perhaps she had chosen the wrong time to tell him this. She had just walked into the house after her evening class and found him seated in the drawing room. The whiskey level in the bottle indicated that he had been drinking for a while. It was only eight o'clock.

'Tired of me already or are you planning to leave and run away, Rhea?'

'You're drunk. We'll talk when you're sober.'

'I am as sober as I can ever be. Tell me, are you running away from me? You might as well because let me tell you… I have no room in my life for Florence Nightingale.'

She felt trapped. No matter what her answer was, he was going to spew more verbal venom on her.

'No, I'm not running away from you. I just wanted to see my parents.'

'So you can complain to them about me? Go and don't come back.'

'You have no idea what you're saying. We'll talk in the morning,' Rhea said and moved in the direction of the bedroom.

Amar swiftly got up and stood in front of her, blocking the way. 'Where do you think you're going? I know exactly what I'm saying. Don't you dare use that superior tone with me.'

Folding her arms in front of her, Rhea stood there without saying another word. There was no point in arguing with him when he was drunk. But her silence infuriated him even further. Amar threateningly moved closer towards her and grabbed her shoulder with one hand. With the other, he picked up the whiskey bottle and asked her to drink from it.

'Amar, I don't want to drink and I don't like whiskey. Please don't do this.'

'Drink or I'll smash this bottle on your head right now.'

'No, you won't,' said Rhea, softly.

'You have no idea.' He matched her soft tone with an evil smile and then shouted, 'DRINK.'

Cringing, she took the bottle from him with hands that were shivering and took a swig.

'More.'

She took another small sip even as tears trickled down her cheeks.

'Keep drinking till I tell you to stop.'

As Amar kept bullying her further, fear gave way to anger. Rhea couldn't take it anymore. She dropped the whiskey bottle to the ground and there was a shattering sound. Hardly had the sound subsided when she heard another. This time, it was much closer to her ears. It had all happened so fast that by the time Rhea realised that Amar had slapped her across her face, he had already caught hold of her hair and was dragging her towards the sofa. Pushing her backwards with force, he menacingly said, 'Don't ever do that again or you'll live to regret it. Do you hear? Answer me.'

'Yes.'

'That's better. Now go to the room and wait for me.'

Rhea was numb. She got up and walked to the bedroom, unaware of the bloody footprint she left behind as the glass cut into her feet.

This is the last time he's ever doing this to me, she thought, glancing sideways at him before entering the room. That's when Rhea saw him chugging away from another bottle as if there was no tomorrow. Even in her wildest dreams, she hadn't imagined that he would turn out like this. Her life had gone from an extreme high to a bottomless low in a matter of three months.

Amar had finished most of the second bottle when he stumbled into the bedroom. She kept her eyes tightly shut as she felt him get into bed. Luck favoured Rhea. Thereafter, there was no movement from his side of the bed. He had passed out.

Rhea quickly picked up her phone and tiptoed outside. Closing the main door behind her, she went downstairs and hailed a taxi. Aditi was the only person she needed right now.

'Where are you, Adu? Can I come over? Are Megha and Ishita home? I need to see you urgently.'

Thankfully, Aditi said that both the girls were out and would be home late. She hung up and gave the driver directions.

When Aditi opened the door for her, Rhea couldn't stop the tears from falling. Soon enough, violent sobs racked her body, leaving Aditi even more bewildered.

'Shhhhh! It's gonna be okay, Rhea. What happened?'

Rhea recounted the horror that she had been dealing with whenever Amar took to the bottle. It had started with small jibes and verbal assaults but today he had crossed the line.

'My god! What a jerk he's turned out to be. He has a serious problem. What I can't understand is why you've waited for things to hit rock bottom before talking to me. What do you want to do now?'

'I have to tell my parents. I will not be one of those wives who get beaten up by an alcoholic husband. I will not.'

Gurleen was speechless when she heard. She hugged Rhea tight as tears trickled down her cheeks, each teardrop filled with sorrow and pain. Jaspal showed a lot of strength in receiving this piece of news, considering that Rhea was the apple of his eye and he couldn't even bear the thought of anyone hurting her.

The mess that emerged over the next few days was far better than what her life would have been if she had stayed married to Amar.

This would be yet another scar in Rhea's life, setting plenty of tongues wagging. It didn't matter that she wasn't at fault here. She would have to face the consequences and live with it forever.

A broken engagement at 15, a broken heart at 22 and a broken marriage at 24! What more was in store for her? It was as if the universe had conspired to add melodrama and catastrophes to her life. Never had Rhea imagined that her life would mirror a tacky B-grade Bollywood movie from the '80s.

11

Mumbai Butterfly

Rhea's life had turned upside down. After the marriage debacle, she had gone back to Jalandhar to spend some time with her parents.

Aditi called her up everyday and continuously coaxed her to return to Mumbai. But Rhea was not ready and besides, she wanted to be with her family. Preet and Geet kept her entertained and she was grateful to have them around. She also looked forward to her daily chats with Aditi. It made her feel connected to the outside world.

'Are you serious? He asked you out? Already? He's hardly known you for a month! What exactly did he say? What was your reply?' Rhea was shooting questions at Aditi over the phone.

'Calm down, woman! I'll tell you everything!'

Over the last month, ever since their studies had concluded, Megha, Aditi and Ishita had been busy looking for a job. They had eventually been hired as interns in different advertising agencies in Mumbai.

It had only been a couple of weeks since Aditi had joined her new office and she was now telling Rhea that a colleague had asked her out.

'Come on, Adu! Spill the beans!' demanded Rhea.

'Well, I've been telling you how Vivaan has been following me around like a puppy in office. Today we went out for a drink, which is when he asked me out. I like him but I told him it was too soon for us to get into a relationship. We hardly know each other. He was cool about it and said he was prepared to wait until I was ready.'

'That is awesome! Find out as much as you can about him. Just make sure he's a nice guy and don't give him an opportunity to take advantage of you in any way. You know where men think from, right?'

'Yes, Mother! Can you stop being overprotective?' teased Aditi, aware that Rhea was only speaking from her personal experience.

'Just saying! No lecture!'

Rhea was glad that Aditi had found someone who made her happy. It had been more than two years since she and Jaskaran had stopped dating.

Suddenly, Rhea missed having Rohan in her life. They had not been in touch after their final break-up. She wondered if he knew about her disastrous and brief marriage. But it wasn't wise to let her thoughts veer towards him, never mind how tempting it was to get in touch while she was in Jalandhar.

After moping over what had happened for three weeks, Rhea decided it was time to head back to Mumbai and start working. She didn't see the point of sitting in Jalandhar and wasting any more time.

Convincing her parents wasn't tough. They both understood that she had to face the world and stand on her own feet. Thankfully, Gurleen had mellowed down.

By the time Rhea joined the girls in Mumbai, Aditi and Megha had settled well into their jobs, whereas Ishita had quit after a month. 'The amount they were paying me was even less than what I spent to reach the office. It didn't make sense,' explained Ishita when Rhea asked.

Rhea was glad that at least now she and Ishita could meet people and explore work opportunities together. It was tough finding a job! They went through all the contacts on their phone to check if anyone could help.

Rhea came to one name and paused. Rohit Khanna. Naaahh! Of all the people in the world, she couldn't call *him* and ask for help or advice. He might still think she was a bitch of the first order for breaking up with Rohan. And she didn't know if he had heard about her marriage fiasco.

Next!

She went through her list again but couldn't see anyone she hadn't called already. She came back to Rohit. Maybe Ishita could help her decide.

'Ishita, I was thinking…should I call up Rohit and seek his advice? You remember him, right? He's Rohan's friend and my senior from school. He's been working here for the last two years, in the media I think. Maybe he can give us some leads or even contacts. What do you think?' asked Rhea, tentatively.

'If you think he can help us, why not? We have to start earning soon. I don't want to live off my parents' money for much longer. Call him and ask if we can meet him.'

Ishita, 'The Practical One', could always be counted on to solve a dilemma.

Nervously, Rhea went to the balcony to make the call. She disconnected twice before finally letting it connect.

One ring! Two rings! Three! Four! Five! Six! Seven! No reply! She heaved a sigh of relief and disconnected the line.

Five minutes later, her phone rang! 'Rohit Khanna' was blinking on the screen! *Shit!* She ran to the balcony and answered on the fourth ring.

'Hi, Rohit! How are you? I hope I didn't disturb you.'

'Rhea? What a surprise! No, you didn't. What's up?'

'All good. Actually, I called to ask you a few things about work. I was wondering if my friend and I could come and meet you one of these days.'

Don't mention Rohan and don't mention my marriage. Please! Please! Please! Rhea was holding her breath.

'Sure. Why not? Can you come over to my office tomorrow afternoon, around 2.30?'

She heaved a sigh of relief. 'We can come to your office. Can you please text me the address?'

'Sure. See you tomorrow then.'

'Thank you so much. See you.' She hung up before the taboo topic could come up.

The last time she had spoken to him was when Rohan was on the train leaving for Jalandhar after their break-up. Rhea wondered what Rohit would be thinking at that moment.

She remembered the last time she had seen him in person. It was outside the boys' hostel a couple of years ago when she had gone to meet Rohan. Rhea remembered that she had felt a bit self-conscious that day because Rohan had been in 'PDA mode'.

Then another thought struck her. What if Rohit called Rohan and told him about her call? *But so what*? She needed to move on in life and stop thinking so much. Rhea pushed these thoughts aside. There was no point in thinking about the past.

The next afternoon, Ishita and Rhea went to meet Rohit at his office. Rhea was nervous but thankfully the meeting wasn't as dramatic as the scenarios she had been conjuring up in her head. He gave them sensible advice and a few pointers on how to find the right client servicing job in a good advertising agency and gave them a few contacts too. It was as professional a meeting as it could be. He didn't ask her anything about Rohan, her marriage or any other personal matter.

'He was so sweet and helpful,' Ishita told Rhea once they left his office.

'He was. Now I just hope his advice helps us.'

It took Ishita another two weeks and Rhea a few more days than that to finally get internships in different firms. Rohit had never called her back to find out if she had found work and she was slightly disappointed at that.

Why do I have such expectations from him? He did me a favour by meeting me. Am I really expecting him to molly-coddle me? It isn't even like we were once really good friends.

She squashed the disappointment in her heart and chided herself. Rohit was soon forgotten.

Rhea's first job at Radical Minds, an advertising firm, was very demanding. Before she knew it, she was spending almost 13 hours in office during the first six months, which was the ever-so-critical probation period.

Radical Minds was one of the top homegrown ad agencies in India and Rhea quickly learnt the ropes under the able leadership of her maverick boss and company founder, Vikram Pushkar. She also realised that Client Servicing was her calling. She was good at convincing people and pitching ideas and was determined to make a good impression on her colleagues and boss. Vikram had a towering personality (literally, too, he was six feet five inches tall) and eyes that shone as bright green stars on a perfectly chiselled Greek God-like face. He saw the promise in her and took her under his wing. She was a fast learner and with her hard work and dedication, soon also became the darling of the office. There was a paradigm shift in her attitude and her confidence level soared even higher when Vikram started taking her along for important client meetings.

Whether it was a pitch for a new FMCG client or a contract re-negotiation, Rhea accompanied Vikram. When she found out that there were rumours in office about their equation with each other, it came as a surprise largely because it was a figment of someone's vivid and overactive imagination. The fact that Vikram was 11 years older than her and a notorious serial dater did not help. But he had never made a move on her so the gossipmongers had got it horribly wrong this time round. Her admiration towards her boss was confined to his negotiation skills at meetings, although she had to admit he was easy on the eyes too. But the thought of them being a couple had never really crossed her mind. While she was somewhat amused, she learnt to look the other way when it came to idle chatter. It was a waste of time. She loved her work and her aim was to prove to her parents and society in general that she could stand on her feet.

One night, Vikram and Rhea were sitting in his cabin after office hours, going over a pitch. Vikram was personally involved because it was for the agency's biggest client—Indian Premier Paints, which was planning a complete overhaul with a new brand identity and logo.

'I love the energy you exude. I knew there was a spark in you and I was not wrong. You are a very smart girl.'

Rhea just stared at him. This praise had come out of the blue. 'Thank you, Vikram. Coming from you, it means a lot. I think we're almost done with preparing for tomorrow's meeting. We should get going now. I will run this by Tapan first thing in the morning before the meeting.'

His body language suddenly changed as his voice took on a huskier note. 'Yes, please do that, darling.'

Noticing the sudden change in his demeanour, Rhea was on alert. As she made eye contact with him, he locked his gaze with hers and refused to look away. Mesmerised, she stared back. She could almost read the tempestuous thoughts in his eyes as he slowly got up from his chair and walked purposefully towards her.

Suddenly, there seemed to be a distinctive energy crackling in the room and Rhea had an ominous feeling. Everyone else had left office by now. She was nervous and wanted to get out.

Vikram sensed her apprehension. Not breaking eye contact for even a second, he pulled her up from her chair and held her hands.

'You are so beautiful, so intoxicating. A sweet little devil with so much fire inside…'

'Umm, tomorrow is a big day for us. I think I should leave.'

'Shhh.. Don't talk, sweetheart.'

Rhea had a strange sensation in the pit of her stomach. Why was she drawn to him like a moth to a flame? A small voice inside her was saying that all this was wrong, that it would ruin everything, but she was beyond listening. After all the crap that life had thrown in her face over the last few years, she deserved to have some fun! It was frisky business, she knew, but sanity could return later.

He kissed her mouth thoroughly, leaving her begging for more. His ran his hands wildly over her body and soon they were lost in a whirlwind of passion.

Vikram insisted they go back to his place but the words of advice from her mother came rushing back to haunt Rhea. She fought it with all her might even as Vikram's hands were caressing her back. At one point, the lure of the unknown was so powerful that the advice conveniently tucked itself into her blind spot. And then she gave in to temptation, completely.

Rhea felt as if she had needed this adrenalin kick in the form of Vikram to bring her life back on track. She had to forget about her bitter past.

In office, they tried to be as professional as they could.

'I have to control myself from touching you when you give me those lingering looks in office. And if you keep at it, one of these days a huge dose of PDA is bound to happen. Then don't blame me,' he told her one day and she smiled.

The client meetings, brainstorming sessions, after-work parties and award functions continued to build Rhea's confidence. She became one with this new world and just like that, the caterpillar from Jalandhar had morphed into a Mumbai butterfly.

12

C'est La Vie

2004
Mumbai

Rhea hung on to Vikram's every word as gospel and their little tryst went on for a few months. He wined and dined her, showered her with sweet-nothings and she soared, believing herself in love.

Despite all that she had gone through, at heart she was still a young girl who wanted someone to make her feel special. Vikram was doing just that.

At office, she wasn't spared from the clichéd allegations. 'She's sleeping her way to the top!' 'She's loose.' 'She doesn't know he's going to drop her like a hot potato soon enough.' The lines got tackier and nastier by the day.

Tapan Chatterjee, the head of the creative department, was the only person Rhea felt she could confide in. He was 35 years old, had more hair on his face than head and was always to be seen in rugged pants and a faded T-shirt. Rhea looked up to him for his unique way of thinking.

When she told him about the latest nasty gossip she had overheard about herself, Tapan told her to be pragmatic. 'Why do you care? Let barking dogs bark.'

'You do know that the correct phrase is: let sleeping dogs lie.'

He arched one eyebrow in a way that only he could and said, 'Now is not the time to give me a lesson in English!'

Rhea's expression sobered. She knew he was going to give her some *gyaan*. 'Grow up, Rhea. If you start getting bothered about what people say about you, you'll never be able to live the way you want to. Stop living in wonderland. Everyone you come across is not a friend so don't be surprised when they don't act like it. And as far as Vikram is concerned, don't get too involved with him. It's not like I need to tell you that he has the reputation of a Casanova. And he has a foolproof escape strategy to get out of his relationships whenever he feels like it.'

'What kind of foolproof escape strategy?'

'He's known to take out the my-childhood-girlfriend-is-back-in-my-life card in order to get out of a relationship and it's worked for him every single time. You enamour him today but it won't last forever. It's happened before and I've seen some girls cry and lose their sanity when he dumps them unceremoniously. And when that day comes in your life, you will feel stupid and pained because in the end, it was you who gave him that power. Just don't let him hurt you. Okay?'

She sighed, not completely wanting to believe what he was saying. *Vikram wouldn't do that to me*, she thought even as Tapan continued, 'All I'm saying is that proximity of the closest kind with the boss doesn't necessarily culminate into anything serious and we know Vikram's reputation. You're a novelty for him right now. Tomorrow he'll find someone else. You won't even realise how swiftly you'll be out of his life, just like a fool's mate.'

'Fool's mate?'

One eyebrow went up again as he looked at her. 'That's checkmate in just two moves. Clearly, you don't know a thing about chess. But that's beside the point. What I'm trying to say is, you're still young so don't get embroiled in the affairs of the heart and believe yourself to be in love with him. Just have a good time like he is and move on when you want to. There's no love in the ad world. Stop being so serious about every person you come across. They only want one thing: to get into your pants. Don't give your heart to them. It's not worth it. Only you will be hurt. So take a hold of your life and be practical.'

How well he knew her! Rhea also remembered giving similar advice to Aditi when Vivaan was wooing her not so long ago. She wondered why she was unable to apply the same counsel when it came to her own life.

'I'm so disillusioned now. You should have let me live the dream for some more time before giving me a rude wake-up call.' Rhea feigned hurt!

'*C'est la vie,* darling! *C'est la vie*!'

And such is love! At 24, Rhea thought that life was extremely complicated. If she had known then that a decade later, complicated would take on a whole new meaning and come accessorised with insecurity, uncertainty and a feeling of worthlessness, she wouldn't have thought of her current situation as being all that bad.

Rhea's phone was ringing, shaking her out of her reverie. After checking who it was, she was in half a mind to ignore it but couldn't. With a little nudge from Tapan, she finally answered.

'*Sat Shri Akal,* Mumma! How are you?' She stepped outside office to talk to her mother peacefully.

Rhea lit a cigarette and tried to concentrate on the information overload from the other side. A tiny sense of guilt reared its head because she was smoking while talking to the mother. Her religion prohibited her from smoking. But then, even alcohol was prohibited and she had seen her father and uncles guzzle bottle after bottle! She quashed that guilt and concentrated on what Gurleen was saying.

It had been almost a year since her marriage to Amar. The divorce had come through six months ago and now her parents wanted her to meet someone else.

'Yes, I know who you're talking about. Okay, Ma, SMS me his email ID and I will add him.'

Rhea didn't have the heart to crush their hopes. She hung up and went back inside, where she knew Tapan would be waiting to hear what happened. He was the only person in office who knew about her marriage. She hadn't even confided in Vikram.

'What's up? Mommy pressuring you to learn cooking?' Tapan was grinning like a Cheshire cat; he had found his entertainment for the day.

'Shut up! Why must you indulge in schadenfreude?'

It was Tapan's turn to look flummoxed. 'Shady freedom? What does that mean?'

Rhea was laughing. 'Google it, Mr. Creative Director.'

'Forget it! Sounds liberating, whatever the hell it means and besides, who has the time? So tell me, what happened?'

'They want me to meet a guy. To top it all, I can't even tell them about Vikram or they'll come here on the next flight and marry me off to him. Can you imagine that? It will be hilarious!'

'Fuck all that! Tell me about this boy that Mother India told you about.'

'It's a schoolmate of mine from Jalandhar, Siddharth Sood.'

'Okay! How old is he?'

'I think he's 28 or 29 and based in Canada. His parents moved to Mumbai a few years ago and now he's coming to India for a holiday.'

'I can't understand why these people choose arranged marriages. Don't they have girlfriends in Canada or the US or wherever else in the world they are?'

'Who knows, he might already have a girlfriend there but agreed to meet me to please his parents. Look at me, I may be in an odd relationship with Vikram but eventually I will end up meeting Siddharth or whoever else my parents want me to meet.'

'What's the first step?'

'MSN Messenger! They want me to add him and chat a bit. I'm told we should get to know each other a little bit before we meet.'

'Add him now! Let's see if he's online. What's his email?'

'Why are *you* so excited? You just want to have fun at my expense, Taps. I don't have his email yet. Mom is going to send it to me.'

'Just marry him and settle down in Kannedaa like a good girl!'

'Please! Let's get back to work. Too much faffing around has happened, don't you think, Mr. Chatterjee?'

He winked at her and left. As soon as she was alone in her cubicle, Rhea googled 'Siddharth Sood'.

'Gotcha!' Tapan popped in from behind and laughed when he saw her computer screen. 'I knew it! I knew it! You sly little thing! Any dirt? Come come, tell tell!'

Rhea blushed at being caught but she might as well dig up the dirt with Tapan around so he could give her some perspective. 'Alright, my partner in crime. Let's get on with it.'

'Oh! Here, open this link. Do you know what he looks like? He has such a common name and this search has thrown up so many different results.'

Rhea's memory of Siddharth dated back almost a decade and she had only hazy recollections.

'Yes! Found him. This is him! Not bad, *na*? What say you? What is this Fotki.com that he has a profile on? I've never heard of it.' Rhea's curiosity was getting the better of her.

'Hold your horses, woman! I don't understand this social networking business but it must be something like those other things, Orkut, Hi5 and what-not-dot-coms. Check the photographs he's uploaded.'

For the next 15 minutes, Tapan and Rhea browsed through Siddharth's profile. They found some pictures of him at parties and Rhea couldn't help but notice that the girls he was with were really pretty. There was one particular girl who kept coming up in the photographs and Tapan noticed this too.

'This one here has to be the hidden *firangi* girlfriend that he can't bring home to his parents,' Tapan told her.

'Shut up! Do you really think so?'

'She could well be. Never rule out any possibility. You need to be careful that he doesn't keep you in the dark about anything, Rhea. Ask questions.'

'Yes, I will. Now let's get back to work. I'm feeling guilty about doing this on office time.'

Just then, Vikram walked into her cubicle and she quickly shut the browser window. Tapan high-fived him and left, and Vikram beckoned Rhea to his cabin.

'There's no better way to put this so I'll be direct. I am getting engaged next month. She's my childhood sweetheart and she relocated from Australia a few weeks back. We've met a couple of times recently and it was like we had never been apart.'

What the fuck! Rhea's jaw dropped. It was happening to her. Just like Tapan had said it would. She was shocked that the legend of his break-up strategy was true. What was she supposed to say to him, *Thanks and have a good life?*

'We won't be able to see each other anymore but I hope this doesn't change anything at work. I really value you as an employee.'

'Wow! No, of course not! Don't be silly. Congratulations! True love is hard to find these days. It does come as a surprise, though. But don't worry about me.'

Rhea wasn't sure which part of her reply answered his question. Her brain was clouding up and she needed to get out of his cabin before she blabbered something idiotic. She needed to calm down.

Play!
Why, this car is automatic
It's systematic, it's hydromatic
Why, it's greased lightning
Greased lightning!
Ohhhhh! Stop! Now is not the time.

She managed to walk out of his cabin calmly but her mind was still talking to her. *It's okay. I am all right. I'm feeling better now. Baby steps! Baby steps!* After rock-and-rolling into *Greased Lightning*, her mind was now quoting Govinda's dialogue from a *masala* Bollywood movie. If this was not a sign of lunacy, she didn't know what was!

There was only one person she needed right now and she sought him out. Wasn't it past 7 p.m? She wanted to leave office right away.

'Taps! Let's go for a drink. I really need a stiff one right now and many more after that.'

'Let's go, kiddo. I was just finishing for the day.' No questions asked. She loved that about him.

Her favourite joint, Café Mondegar, was the closest to their office. It was unassuming, even with its artistic walls and vintage atmosphere. Rhea liked the buzz there as much as the music that flowed from the old jukebox, which stood at the far end of the room.

Tapan was ordering a beer pitcher.

'I think I want something stronger like a Long Island Iced Tea,' said Rhea in a daze.

'Hello! Are you drunk already or did you forget that Monde's serves only beer and wine? We shall stick to beer since we know what wine does to you.'

'How silly of me to forget. Okay, uncle, as long as I'm allowed to drink as much as I want, beer will do just fine! And please also order fish fingers.'

'Fish have fins, not fingers!'

'A very bad one, Taps!'

'The pressure to live up to your expectations will kill me!'

In the midst of this rather stupid banter, which was doing a good job of distracting her, he placed their order and sat quietly next to her for what seemed like an eternity.

'Aren't you going to ask me what happened?'

'You're going to tell me anyway, aren't you? I'm listening. Whenever you're ready.'

'Hmm! Let the beer come.'

Half a glass of beer later, Rhea finally spoke again, 'You were right. The childhood girlfriend has arrived. I wish I had paid heed to your advice.'

'I'll save you the pain by not saying I told you so. But with you being an employee, somewhere I expected him to act differently. Did he really think you wouldn't get to know?'

Rhea's beer had now started talking. 'That son of a bitch! What an asshole! And I'm so stupid. He didn't even think that I deserved an original story? Am I not worthy of that at least? Why did he not make an effort to cook up a new story to tell me? He could have told me that he was gay or that he'd had a child marriage and his wife had just come of age! Couldn't he?'

Rhea went bottoms up on her next glass and was laughing at her own jibe till the tears rolled.

'You've totally lost the plot now. *Tum usko apna* life *aur* mind *se tada-tadi* push *kar*. *Uska* name *bhi toh wohi hai na*, Vikram Pushkar.'

Tapan's silly words stopped her tears as if by magic and Rhea laughed. '*Arrey, Babu Moshai*, stick to English. You've totally slaughtered the already lame joke by explaining it.'

Tapan winked at her and continued. 'Forget about Vikram. He was never worth it. It's not like you were in love with him.'

'Of course I was, I mean I am, in love with him. I don't date men just randomly. I just might not have said it out loud.'

'Oh, don't kid yourself, babe! You're in love with the idea of being in love.'

'*Et tu*, Brute?'

'Damn right, Caesar.

'Okay, now that hurt. It was probably true when I was engaged at 15 and in love with the idea of being in love. Not now...now I'm older!'

'But not necessarily wiser! And engaged at 15! Are you serious? Girl, what all have you gone through?'

Rhea was somewhat surprised that she had missed out on telling Tapan about this earlier. 'Now that's a story you must hear. I also assure you these drunken ramblings will be my dignity destroyer but please judge me not.'

'Okay, my drama queen. Please to be proceeding.' Tapan was ready to hear anything that would take Rhea's mind off Vikram.

'So I was engaged to this guy, Happy Singh...don't laugh!'

'I'm not laughing. Continue.'

'So during the time I was engaged to him, I had once lied to my parents saying I was going for an overnight studying session to Aditi's place and instead went for a friend's farewell party, a boy's. The guys were all merrily high and asked me for Happy's phone number. I refused knowing that they would be upto no good. But eventually after a lot of pestering, I gave in when Aadish promised me that it would only be a blank call to hear how he sounded. They wouldn't utter a word.'

'And let me guess...they spoke shit.'

'Well, my friends only wanted to bug Happy with a blank call but when some other boys from school, who were also at the party, got to know about it things got out of hand. Happy had answered and the boys had snatched the cordless out of Aadish's hand and went on a rampage. They were so drunk that they had no idea what they were saying. They made fun of his name and cracked idiotic *sardar* jokes on him.'

'But if Happy spoke to some random boys, how did he know that you were involved?'

'Because some ass was chanting away "Oh, Rhea! Yes, Rhea!" in the background. When I finally managed to grab the phone from one of their hands and tried to speak to Happy, he just said, "I don't know what that was all about and I'm not even interested in finding out. God alone knows what you're doing. I didn't expect you to be like this."'

'How reckless of those boys. They put you in a lot of trouble.'

'Yeah! Shit happens in life. Those boys did apologise to me later when they got to know that my engagement had been called off. But anyway, I don't regret any of it. Everything happens for a reason. So Taps, now you belong to a secret society of people who know my secret.'

While reliving some of the old pain, the new pain was forgotten, if only for a little while. She had lost count of how many mugs of beer she downed that night. By the time they were ready to leave Monde's, she had difficulty standing straight, let alone walk. Tapan guided her to a cab and got in the back seat beside her.

'I can go home on my own. Really! You don't need to come with me.'

But he would hear none of it. Rhea put her head on his shoulder and was glad he was with her. She hoped the girls wouldn't be home. She didn't want to talk to any of them right now and have them telling her what a fool she had been.

'Fool's mate. Checkmate. Stalemate. Climate. Penultimate. Fornicate. No! No fornicate does not rhyme. Ha! Ha! Ha!' She was blabbering in her drunken stupor and Tapan shook his head in dismay.

Rhea must have dozed off because the next thing she knew, he was shaking her awake.

'Don't be so hard of yourself, kiddo. These things happen in life and it only makes you stronger. Learn from your mistakes and move on. Be careful not to repeat them. Now go get some sleep and pop two Disprins in the morning if you have a headache.'

'I'm sorry you had to listen to all my crap. You know I love you.'

'Love you too! Now go!'

If ever there was a gentleman in the giddy world of advertising, here he was. Rhea felt lucky to have a sounding board like him.

13

Mr. Perfect? Mr. Right?

The Siddharth distraction in her life couldn't have come at a more opportune time. She needed to forget that shallow ass, Vikram.

In office, she was successful in avoiding a run-in with Vikram because he was in the middle of finalising a merger with an international agency and was mostly out of town. However, she knew that it was time for her to move on and thus Rhea began sending her updated resume to friends and colleagues.

Rhea had added Siddharth on Instant Messenger and he had accepted her request almost immediately. The time difference meant they often chatted at odd hours; sometimes, Rhea would be awake till the wee hours of the morning, waiting for him to take a break at work so they could talk. Their conversations would range from their taste in music and films to books and other topics. While Rhea was a voracious reader of fiction, he devoured pages on management, business and leadership. She liked the latest pop music; he was more inclined towards jazz and country. While she eagerly lapped up all the mush that Bollywood and Hollywood had to offer, he preferred world cinema. Rhea thought their differing tastes were a good thing. If they were to end up together, both of them would definitely learn new ways of living.

When it came to food, their palettes matched. Whether it was Italian, Mexican, Chinese, Thai or Burmese that was on the menu, both could be counted on to wipe their plates clean. Of course, good ol' Indian food was always welcome. Siddharth was a fan of south Indian fare while Rhea enjoyed traditional Punjabi *khana—tadka maar ke*.

Early on in her chats with him, Rhea had thought it appropriate to come clean about her past—the broken engagement at 15 and the doomed marriage the previous year. Siddharth had been sympathetic and lauded her for taking a tough call and getting out of the marriage. She was relieved. Maybe being a divorcee had slowly stopped being a taboo.

Rhea was almost dozing off one night, when her laptop pinged. That 'ping' sound had now replaced alarm clocks in her life and she was wide-awake in a jiffy. When she saw Siddharth's message, her heart started beating a little faster.

'Hey, sleepyhead!'

'Hey, yourself! And as if you can see me! I'm not sleepy ☺'

'What are you doing at this late hour?'

'Waiting for Godot!'

'Hahaha!'

'What are you upto?'

'I just got out of a meeting and saw you online so thought I'd say hi. And I have some news for you.'

'Oh! What is it?'

'I'll be in India next month.'

She sat up in her bed, her joy knowing no bounds. *Really? Oh my God! Oh my God! He's finally coming to India. I'm going to meet him at last. Will he like me? Will I like him? But I already like him. Don't I? What are we going to talk about? Fuck! What am I going to wear? I need to go shopping. I need to get a haircut, facial, manicure, pedicure... what else?* It was a good thing he couldn't see her or else he would think she was a psycho.

The next message she typed showed none of the excitement she was feeling.

'That's nice! How long will you be here?' *Oh, how 'propah' I sound! If only he knew what I was feeling.*

'Nice? That's it? What a lukewarm response. I thought you would be excited.'

Oh! You have no idea! 'Of course I'm happy. The true tone of what one says cannot be interpreted over chat!'

Damn! What am I saying? That I'm way too excited about meeting him? Just stop blabbering!

'Haha! I get it. Anyway! I'll let you know my travel plans soon. Now I need to run into a meeting so catch you later.'

'Sure! Have a nice day! Ciao!'

She was dying to call one of her girlfriends and tell them this exciting news. Alas! It was way past midnight and there wasn't half a chance that any one of them would be awake.

It had been a few months since the four girls had gone their separate ways from their two-bedroom apartment in Bandra. Aditi and Vivaan had rented an apartment together and had been going steady for about eight months. Megha had quit her job and moved to Delhi and Ishita was staying with her brother, Ranbir, who had recently been transferred to Mumbai. Rhea had found herself a quaint little studio apartment in Versova.

She would have to wait until morning to tell the girls about Siddharth. After the Vikram debacle in her life, her friends had been her support system and so far they had liked whatever she had told them about Siddharth.

Rhea woke up with the sound of the phone ringing. She tried to ignore it but it was her mother. '*Sat Sri Akal*, Mumma!'

'*Sat Sri Akal, beta*! Did I wake you up?'

'No! I was just getting up. What happened?'

Before Rhea could update her about her own conversation the previous night, Gurleen told her that Siddharth's parents were keen to meet her soon.

'Your father and I have decided to come to Mumbai for a couple of days and then we can go meet them.'

'Mom, I chatted with Siddharth last night. He is coming to India next month. Don't you think we should wait for him and then meet his parents?'

'Oh, is he? That's very good news. Let me check with his parents and update you.'

Later that day, Gurleen called Rhea to tell her that Siddharth's parents had insisted they all meet once before he came to India. Rhea found it a bit strange but didn't really have a say in the matter. It was decided that Gurleen and Jaspal would come down over the weekend.

That night, she didn't see Siddharth on chat. She stayed online for a few hours but there was no sign of him. Suddenly, there was a ping on her laptop.

'Hey! How are you? Working late?'

Rohit? Why was he messaging her so late at night? She was in no mood to get into a conversation with him. Disappointed at Siddharth's virtual absence, Rhea chose not to reply and logged off.

The next day, she signed into her IM account from office in the hope of finding Siddharth online but he wasn't logged in.

Rhea was just about to log off when Rohit messaged again. 'Yo, Rhea! Wassup? How you doing?'

It would be rude to ignore him twice in a row and so she decided to reply. 'Hi! I'm good! How are you?'

'Great, eh. How is life? What are you upto?'

'Life's good :) presently at work.'

'You seem to be working really hard. You must be busy; I'll speak with you later.'

'Yeah, well, not that busy, but just trying to wrap up work so I can leave office.'

'Oh, cool! I was also leaving so I just thought I'd say hi to you before I go.'

'Okay, later then.'

'Sure. You take care. Catch you soon! Cheers'

'Yup! You too. Ciao'

She still couldn't shake off the strange feeling she had about him messaging her. Why all of a sudden? What kind of a lame-ass conversation was she having with him? *Catch you soon?* As if!

She logged off and forgot all about him. Her mind was on the impending meeting with Siddharth's parents. Jaspal and Gurleen were to arrive on Friday and they were all going to his house for dinner on Saturday.

Rhea had last met Simi Aunty almost 10 years ago but now was not the time to go into flashback mode. She had a host of things to do before she met 'the' parents. First, she had to catch up with Aditi and update her. They decided to meet for dinner that night.

'You have disappeared on me! Vivaan keeping you busy these days, huh?'

'I have something to tell you.'

'What? Tell me! Tell me!'

'Viv has asked me to marry him and I said yes!'

'Oh my God! That is wonderful, Adu! I'm so happy for you! Have you guys set the date? Give me all the intricate details.'

Rhea was overjoyed. Over the last few months, she had gotten to know Vivaan and found him to be a genuinely nice guy. She was over the moon that Aditi had found the love of her life.

At the end of the night and many beers later, the girls had related their stories to each other and were happy with the way their lives were panning out—Aditi and Vivaan, Rhea and Siddharth! Perfect didn't even begin to describe it.

The day Rhea was meeting Siddharth's parents arrived way too soon. She was nervous but reminded herself that it was actually not the first time she was meeting them.

While they were on their way, Gurleen was repeating the same instructions she had when they were travelling to Delhi to meet Happy. That memory seemed from another lifetime but Rhea was doing the same thing she had all that time ago; constantly saying 'Yes' to every instruction, until…

'If they ask you about your work, tell them you are just doing timepass and it's nothing that you can't leave after marriage.'

Rhea couldn't believe her ears. She was absolutely disgusted with her mother's way of thinking.

'Timepass? I am not doing timepass, Mumma, and I am good at what I do. Why would I belittle my work?'

'Don't answer back and do as I say.'

Lady Hitler was back! Rhea couldn't understand the world her mother lived in! How could she even say something like that and expect her to agree? She strained to hold her tongue yet again like she had always done in the past. She knew arguing would only make it worse so she decided to take a deep breath and ignore it. Now was not the time to be crabby.

Thankfully, dinner went off well and Siddharth's parents took an instant liking to her. Jaspal and Gurleen told them about her previous unfortunate marriage experience but that was only a formality. They had a circle of friends in Jalandhar and had known about it all. It didn't bother them in the slightest, they said, and Rhea was glad!

The question about her job did arise but Rhea could not get herself to say that she was simply indulging in 'timepass'. She decided to be vague in her reply in order to avoid another lecture from Gurleen.

That night, she met Siddharth online and told him all about the dinner. His parents had also updated him. From then on, time flew and stagnated at the same time. The days were getting closer to his arrival and yet it seemed far away.

They set up a date for the week after he arrived, deciding on the JW Marriot coffee shop as the meeting place. When the day finally dawned, Rhea was so nervous that she couldn't eat.

She tried not to think about her previous arranged marriage rendezvous with Happy, Puneet and Amar. This was different. She and Siddharth were two individuals on a similar wavelength who had had the same kind of upbringing. She could relate to him even though he was a few years older than her.

When she finally started getting to know him, she was completely blown away. He was unlike any man she had ever met. Rhea felt he could take care of her and give her the love and security she craved for. He was perfect, almost too good to be true. She had a strong sense that this was meant to be.

The conversation varied from their early life in Jalandhar, his job and his life in Canada to her work and personal life in Mumbai. By the time they bid each other goodbye, Rhea believed herself to be head over heels in love with him.

14

Matrimonial Mocktale

2005
Mumbai

Rhea had finally moved on from Radical Minds and joined a firm called Transcendental Misfits as Senior Account Executive in the client servicing department. She was working in the same agency as Sagar Mittal, a well-known creative genius in advertising circles.

She had stayed in touch with some of her colleagues at Radical Minds but their meetings were few and far between. Tapan was the only one she spoke to regularly and truly missed.

Meanwhile, Aditi and Vivaan got married with stylish aplomb. They had a fun wedding in Goa where only a few close friends and family were invited. It was unlike the typical Big Fat Indian Wedding!

It was also a reunion of sorts. A motley crowd comprising their friends from Jalandhar and Mumbai had gathered for the wedding. Rhea was ecstatic to be with the gang for her best friend's wedding. There hadn't been a happier day in her life.

The wedding day was chaos personified. The ceremony was due to be performed in half an hour and there was no sign of the bride. 'She's hasn't reached the venue yet. She's in the parlour getting ready. Vivaan has already reached. They're going to call for her any minute now.' Megha was giving them updates.

'Oh, oh! Should I reach the venue on Aditi's behalf?' replied Myra. Rhea burst out laughing. In times of pressure and stress, Myra could be counted on to lighten the mood.

But this was not a time for jokes. Aditi had gone to the parlour with one of her cousins. Myra called her up. 'How much more time, Adu? We are all waiting for you. Vivaan has reached.'

'*Usse kehna intezaar kare, yeh dulhan waqt lagayegi.*' Aditi quoted a dialogue from *Kuch Kuch Hota Hai* and Myra rolled her eyes. 'My! My! We have a filmy *dulhan* in the house!'

'Alright! Alright! My saree is being draped now. My hair took so long to get done. Finally I decided not to go with the bun.'

'If you didn't go with the bun, did you go with the bread... sorry...braid?' Myra was in her element!

'Girls, can you please hurry up! Tell Aditi that she has to be here in the next 10 minutes.' Nita Aunty, known for her calm and composed demeanour, was now getting hyper. This was a sureshot sign that things were not to be taken lightly.

Rhea was teary-eyed just thinking about the fact that Aditi would be married in a few hours. Not that this would be a real goodbye for them but send-offs made her emotional.

Aditi and Vivaan were so happy with each other. Rhea hoped she too would find such bliss one day with someone who loved her. She tried not to think of Siddharth. They had only met that one time during his entire trip and Rhea had started thinking something was amiss. However, she hadn't wanted to be a nag and ask him probing questions. She chose instead to come across as the cool one, who couldn't care less. Only she knew how it was eating her from inside and taking away her peace of mind.

What could have gone wrong? Why was he not making another plan to meet her? Before she had known what to make of it, the time had come for him to return to Canada. He had kept in touch but Rhea didn't know what he had in mind.

Tapan's words of advice, coupled with the memory of that girl from the photograph whom they had assumed to be his girlfriend, played an insufferable audio-visual medley in front of her eyes.

2006
Mumbai

Everyone around her was getting married and moving ahead in life and here she was, playing the waiting game. At 26, she was ready for marriage and love and the traditional happily-ever-after, despite all her unpleasant past experiences.

One day, while they were chatting, Rhea decided that the time had come to ask Siddharth some important questions. They had known each other for almost one-and-a-half years now. Her parents kept asking her at regular intervals if they had decided anything and Rhea kept making excuses for Siddharth. Not any more!

'Hi! How have you been? Haven't heard from you in a long time.' Her fingers typed away.

'Yes! I've been travelling. I was in Miami with friends for a holiday.'

No hi! No hello! Nothing! Rhea's overactive imagination could almost see the supposed girlfriend prancing in the famous itsy-bitsy-teenie-weenie-yellow-polka-dot-bikini on the beaches of Miami. She shook her head vigorously as if by doing that the girl's image would automatically delete from her mind.

'That's nice. I hope you had a good time.'

'Yes, I did. Thank you!'

'So, I've been waiting to talk to you about something.'

How she hated doing this.

'Sure. Tell me.'

'My parents have been asking me about us and I don't really know what to tell them. It's been more than a year that we've known each other so they're getting a bit paranoid.'

'I can understand.'

'I don't know where we stand and where we're going from here. I'm not putting any pressure on you but I need to know because I have to tell them something. They want me to meet these other guys since they don't see any progress from our side. Right now I'm not even sure if there is an "us".'

'I don't know what to say. We've hardly spent any time with each other and I find it difficult to make a decision based on just one meeting.'

The audacity! Whose fault was it that we met only once? Rhea was trying hard to control her anger. She couldn't believe what she was hearing but held her tongue.

'Sure. I understand.'

'I am planning to relocate to India very soon. Maybe then we can get to know each other better.'

'When are you planning to move back?'

'Soon enough. There are some things I need to take care of and wrap up before I can leave for good.'

'Cool.'

Rhea latched on to that little glimmer of hope and forgot her anger and frustration. She would make her parents understand. If they had waited for so long, what harm could some more days do?

The 'soon enough' turned into six months and there was still no sign of him coming back. Slowly, Rhea distanced herself. She stopped chatting with him even if she did see him online. He too never took the initiative to strike up a conversation. And just like that, the possibility of 'Rhea and Siddharth' was over, two years after it began.

Nevertheless, the marriage proposals kept piling up, mainly via emails.

Without preamble, parents of random strangers would ask Rhea to send in her photographs, qualifications, and physical features as if she was a display item in a showroom! The only difference was that they didn't ask for guarantees or warranty. Some even asked her if she knew how to drive. *Since when did that become a criterion for marriage? Or were they looking for a driver?*

Many would not go ahead without getting the date, time and place of her birth. Rhea was surprised that a lot of people still believed that the 'stars' of the boy and girl should match. What's more, even Gurleen was still consulting Bittu Maharaj for advice on astrological voodoo!

Disillusioned with men in general, Rhea went through all those meetings with the least interest. Some of the guys her parents were making her meet were just not her type. They were being considered merely because they were open to the idea of marrying a divorcee.

Over the next few months, a few people from her workplace voiced their interest in getting to know her better but Rhea kept them at arm's length because she knew it would be practically impossible to convince her mother to marry her off to someone outside their community. She knew she would eventually lose the battle and, in any case, she did not want to sever ties with her family. So, she went along with the plan that they had in mind for her. First, second, third, fourth...after a while, she lost count of the number of men she was made to meet over the next two years.

The worst dresser ever with the weirdest questions: Pritam Something was the first and only guy that Rhea met without checking out his 'biodata' or having a dekko at his photograph. They decided to meet at Mocha in Churchgate. Rhea reached the café right on time and looked around for him. She gave up after a few minutes and decided to give him a call.

She could hear a phone ringing somewhere and turned around in that direction. When she saw the person she was meant to meet, she immediately hung up and eyed the exit. But Pritam had spotted her by then and there was no way she could make a run for it.

He was wearing a maroon and brown turtleneck sweater (in Mumbai!), which had pillings all over. Rhea's eyes immediately went to his shoes, which had definitely seen better days. As if that wasn't enough, she was further appalled to see that he wore no socks!

What have I got myself into? How am I even going to have a decent conversation with him when the presence of pillings and absence of socks is all that my mind can think of? How can anyone be so unconcerned and lackadaisical in their attitude?

Rhea's thoughts were all over the place and anger was a predominant emotion right now. How could her parents put her in a situation like this?

To make matters worse, he looked flabbergasted when he spotted her dressed the way she was. She was wearing a black sleeveless top, jeans and high heels and had kohl-outlined eyes, glossy lips and she carried a tote bag.

Five minutes into the conversation, he was asking her whether she was religious, if she went to the Gurudwara regularly to pray and if she knew how to cook. Rhea was seriously beginning to wonder if all these men prepared from professionally drawn up questionnaires on 'What to ask an Indian girl on the first meeting for a possible arranged marriage'.

However, the questions that followed thereafter shocked her beyond belief.

'I hope you are not a loony.'

Rhea almost spat out her drink.

'Excuse me? Did you just say "loony"?' Rhea said quickly, grabbing a tissue paper and wiping her lips.

'Yes, that's what I said. I have previously met four girls for marriage and all of them were loony.'

Rhea was amazed. Hardly had she recovered from that, when he fired another salvo.

'I don't like women putting *kajal* in their eyes. If we do get married, you would have to give up *kajal* forever.'

It was not a question and she stared at him blankly, aware more so now of the kohl in her eyes. Her mind refused to believe that there were people like him in this world. When he asked his next question, all Rhea could do was laugh out loud.

'I hope you are not used to the Western style commode toilet because everyone in our house prefers Indian style toilets. And also, no going abroad for honeymoon.'

Toilet and honeymoon commands! Pritam was on a roll (pun intended).

'I do prefer Western toilets. We would have to install a commode in your bathroom if we do get married. For our honeymoon, forget going abroad, we must go to Malgudi.' She replied with a straight face, wanting to add, 'in your dreams'. He looked at her skeptically. She was sure that he would look up Malgudi on the map once their meeting was over.

Rhea didn't know how to get out of the situation without being rude. She toyed with her phone, hoping it would ring, hoping someone would call her so she could slink away from this ordeal. But it remained ominously silent. She quickly blind-typed a message to Tapan from under the table: 'SOS. Call me.'

That Tapan would pull her leg about this for the rest of her life was the least of her concerns right now. She desperately needed to get out of here. And he didn't let her down. Within 20 seconds, her phone was ringing. She answered after apologising to Pritam, saying it was an important call. 'Yes, sir! I've just stepped out for coffee.'

Silence.

'Okay. I'll be in office in 10 minutes. Yes, I understand it's important. I'll be there.'

Tapan was laughing his head off on the other side. She hung up, trying hard to control the urge to join in the laughter. 'I'm really sorry but I have to go. My boss just called to say something urgent has come up. Thank you for the coffee. It was nice to meet you.'

Pritam didn't know what hit him and she was beyond caring. She just knew she had to run for her life! She speed-dialled her father as soon as she stepped out. 'Papa! Never ever ask me to meet a guy without finding out everything about him! Never! I just had the most trying experience ever. This arranged marriage routine will make me a deranged woman if I keep meeting guys like him.'

She recounted whatever had happened and Jaspal was apologetic. However, they soon made light of the situation and were laughing about it. By the end of the conversation, her father was even singing the old Hindi song 'Pritam Aan Milo' in a nasal tone.

'Oh, Papa, you're incorrigible!'

Next!

I want to break free: That famous song by Queen may as well have held true for Virender Something's mother, Jasmeet, and she had no qualms in admitting it to someone who was a prospective daughter-in-law!

Virender was a software engineer. While Rhea didn't find any particularly grating qualities in Virender, Jasmeet was another matter altogether. What Rhea was going to hear next was beyond the realms of her imagination!

'I just want Virender to get married so that his wife can take all the responsibilities off me and I can be free. All my life I have wanted to travel and see new places but I've never been able to because of my elder son. I'm not sure if you know but he is mentally challenged and lives with Viru and me. The boys' father and I are separated.'

Rhea was aghast. Jasmeet was relentlessly painting out her dreams and it was claustrophobic just listening to her. Scenarios started playing in her mind. A mentally challenged brother, a husband who might not speak up for his wife, in-laws who lived separately and a mother-in-law who wanted to spread her wings and fly.

Play!
I believe I can fly
I believe I can touch the sky
Low battery! Please stop!

The claustrophobia gave way to an odd sense of alarm in her mind. It was a sweet deal for everyone except Rhea. For her, it was as raw as it could get. She had to make an exit, pronto!

Her uncle, Surinder, had accompanied her and his expressions alone said he was as appalled as she was when he heard the woman talk. Rhea communicated to Surinder with her eyes that she wanted to make a beeline for the door.

The 'I-want-to-break-free' Jasmeet was still yapping about how she wanted to travel to Kashmir, Shimla and Darjeeling and couldn't wait for her son to be married so she could scoot.

Rhea had heard enough. 'Aunty, I don't mean to be rude and maybe I don't really understand where you're coming from but what you need is a nanny for your older son and not a wife for the younger one. I'm sorry but I'm not interested in this proposal. It was nice to meet you.'

She got up and so did Surinder, who was shocked that Rhea had actually given a piece of her mind to this woman. She didn't even cast a glance at Virender and was out of the door in a flash.

As soon as they got into Surinder's car, they both looked at each other and laughed. 'Mama*ji*! How many specimens will I have to meet before I find the right one?'

Surinder gave her an almost apologetic smile but refrained from answering the question.

Next!

Of BMWs, Porsches and Hookah Bars: This one was a rich spoilt brat whose main hobby seemed to be bragging. One look at him and Rhea knew that he was trouble. Varun Something lived in London and only spoke about 'I, Me and Myself'!

'I love speed! I drive my BMW in London but when I go down to the countryside over the weekend, I take my Porsche.'

'My, my! Aren't we modest?'

Rhea tried the sarcasm card but even that was lost on him. What a 'duh' he was! Money couldn't buy class and here was a living example.

As if that wasn't enough, Rhea found herself listening to his plans for opening a Hookah Bar in Mumbai and how he was scouting for locations.

A Hookah Bar! This was going to be fun. Bring it on.

'Why would you want to open a Hookah Bar in Mumbai when you're based in London? Do you have a partner for the project who can manage the business while you're away?'

It was a logical question.

'It's the 'in-thing' right now in Mumbai, isn't it? Mumbai is cheaper than London, you know, so that's why I want to open it here. I can keep travelling between the two cities.'

'Hmmmpp! Interesting.'

There was no way she was ever marrying him but she was somewhat intrigued at this new specimen she had come across. She decided to quiz him some more, just for the fun of it.

'So what kind of initial capital do you require to open a Hookah Bar?'

He couldn't, for the life of him, hide the fact that the question had totally flummoxed him. Maybe Varun hadn't expected her to ask questions but he recovered quickly and tried to answer. 'Well, it depends on where you want to open it. Prices in the suburbs will differ from prices in town.'

Rhea just about managed to stop herself from rolling her eyes. 'Well, that's obvious! Isn't it? So supposing you want to open it in Bandra, what would be the investment required?'

'You know, I don't really want to get into the details as of now but my team is currently preparing a docket on it. Forget the Hookah Bar, why don't we talk about you?'

While he was giving his ball-talk, an SOS message had been sent to Tapan. It was now becoming a safe exit route from these silly capers she kept marching into.

Eureka. The phone was ringing. Making an excuse, Rhea bid the latest faffer adieu and profusely thanked Tapan for bailing her out yet again.

Rhea felt as if she was destined to meet all the dumb men of the world.

Next!

Punjabi *Swayamvars*: As far as Rhea knew, the concept of a *swyamvar*—an ancient practice of a woman choosing her life partner from a list of suitors—was passé.

She could not, for the life of her, imagine herself going around a hall full of prospective suitors with a garland in hand and choosing someone by putting the garland around his neck.

The vision of Seeta's *swayamvar* from the *Ramayana* TV serial she had seen as a child came to mind. It gave Rhea the creeps.

Nonetheless, the Sikh community was organising *swayamvar*s in different parts of the country. It was a place where single girls and boys came with their families to look for a suitable match. The 'candidates' would all go up on a podium one by one and introduce themselves.

Gurleen had told Surinder about one such *swayamvar* that was scheduled to take place in Mumbai and wanted him to convince Rhea to attend it. When she got to know, she refused point blank.

Many words of wisdom and doses of emotional blackmail later, a rather peeved Rhea finally gave her assent but on the condition that she would not go up on stage and introduce herself. She would be a spectator and choose the guys she wanted to meet, not vice versa.

The word '*swayamvar*' itself was enough to make her nauseous. There was no way that she could tell any of her friends or colleagues about it. Rhea felt as if she was living in two different worlds at the same time.

Of all the boys who spoke on stage that day, there was probably just one, Dilpreet Something, she considered meeting. The lesser said about the rest of the potential *pappu*s, the better.

Gurleen was thrilled even with this sole green light and went right up to his family and introduced herself.

This whole thing was tacky and Rhea's embarrassment knew no bounds. There was no escape in sight this time, not even Tapan.

The *swayamvar* was organised in an open ground so Dilpreet and Rhea decided to take a walk to 'get to know each other'.

His opening lines caught her off guard. He sure didn't believe in wasting time. 'So what are you looking for in your partner?'

Rhea was stumped. What could one possibly say in reply? Who knew how her answer might be judged? It wasn't like she didn't know what she wanted but it was difficult to articulate.

'I don't know…there are so many things but I guess emotional compatibility is most important. What are you looking for?'

'I'm looking for someone who will take care of my family and be my equal.'

'So you're fine with your wife being a working woman and sharing household responsibilities with her when you both come home from work?'

'It depends. She can work from home and do whatever she likes but the family comes first.'

Then don't say shit like you want her to be your equal! Rhea wanted to shout but he was already onto his next question.

'Are you religious?'

Oh! For God's sake (pun intended), what was the connection between marriage, religion, praying and God?

'I am an atheist,' said Rhea with a deadpan expression for shock value.

'What religion is that?'

Fuck! Who was this guy? No, seriously! Who was he?

'An atheist is someone who does not believe in God.'

'You're joking! How can you not believe in God? We owe him everything we have. Our life, our existence…everything!'

'Have you seen him?'

'No, I haven't, but in India, we have such a rich history of Gods and Goddesses. It can't be stupid if everyone believes in religion.'

'Mythology, not history. There's a difference. I never said religion or the people who believe in God are stupid. I respect their views and beliefs but I don't have to accept or abide by them.'

'So you don't pray? Aren't you scared?'

'Scared of what? I don't believe in asking God for things. If everyone had their needs and wants answered, there wouldn't be a single person in the world who wouldn't have what they prayed for. There would be no poverty, no unhappiness, no fights, no famine and no problems. All you had to do was pray and poooof...you would have whatever you wanted. That's what most people do when they pray, right? Ask for things.'

She paused for breath and was surprised when he didn't say anything, so she continued.

'I do believe in a nameless higher power but not in the millions of deities we have. One day, regardless of whether I pray or not, I will die. Everyone has to die. No one knows what lies ahead in the other world. When I come to it, I'll see. Why should I be scared?'

Once the monologue was over, her rational mind said that she had been way too bold.

Not surprisingly, Dilpreet rejected her.

A year later, Rhea got to know from her uncle that Dilpreet had liked another girl at the same *swayamvar* and had married her in a couple of months. Now the girl was filing for divorce even though she was pregnant with his child. They didn't get along.

After finding his partner hastily and jumping into the marriage, the news really didn't really come as much of a surprise! After all, she had also been there, done that! Rhea wondered if Dilpreet had married that girl because he found her to be appropriately religious. All she could do was thank her stars.

Next!

Blasted past: Her parents then introduced her to a guy online. While they both seemed to like each other, the horror of the horoscope played spoilsport.

Kanwaljeet Something's mother said their *kundali*s didn't match whereas Gurleen's Bittu Maharaj gave the proposal his thumbs up. This strange dichotomy regarding the same *kundalis* perplexed Rhea. Maybe there was another reason why his family didn't want to take this proposal forward. Images of her broken engagement and marriage were suddenly astir in her mind. Her past had to be the reason, she decided. There was no other rationale because Kanwaljeet said he liked her but the only reason they couldn't take it forward was because their horoscopes didn't match.

Society would never let her forget, no matter how desperately she wanted to put the past aside. Rhea was getting more and more disillusioned with the idea of marriage.

Next!

Maybe not an ABCD and, then again, maybe: 'She's so choosy. We have seen so many boys till now. She always manages to find fault with them. There will be a time when she has to compromise. I hope it's not too late by then. Everything can't be the way she wants it.'

Rhea wanted to cry when she overheard Gurleen telling Jaspal this on the day they were supposed to meet Gautam Something. She hated the word 'compromise' but what she hated even more was that her parents' ultimate dream remained her marriage, regardless of the ordeals she had already been through.

She thought long and hard. Maybe she was being way too picky-choosy. She decided she would say 'Yes' to this proposal no matter what. How bad could it get? It was one of those days when she lacked any zest for life. She wanted to settle down not because she had found her perfect match but because it was what society 'demanded' and 'expected' of her. The more guys she met, the more cumbersome and disheartening it got. This needed to end.

Gautam was an average-looking guy who came across as very 'propah' from his actions and words. He was based in the US, a graduate of Georgia Institute of Technology with almost eight years of experience in investment banking and he loved photography. He seemed perfect. Rhea was going to marry him if all went well.

Their first meeting was brilliant and they decided to meet again but without their respective families in tow. Rhea was happy with the way things were going.

Two days later, Myra was throwing a Diwali party at her place. Rhea begged off from the party early, saying she had to meet someone.

'You can't leave my party now! The night's still young and so are we!'

'I have to meet someone. My parents have hooked me up with this guy and I'm due to meet him in 20 minutes.'

'Why don't you ask him to join us here? I'm not letting you leave. Call him over.'

Gautam was more than happy to join the party. She introduced him to her friends and he seemed to enjoy himself. The informal setting also made it easy for them to connect. While the alcohol was flowing freely, Rhea chose to sip slowly on her gin and tonic.

This had to be one of the best evenings she'd had in a long time. They laughed, cracked jokes and even connected on topics like travel, photography, nature and art. The more she thought, the more she believed that Gautam would be a great life partner. Thank God he wasn't one of those ABCDs—American Born Confused Desis—that she'd heard so much about.

By the time the party was wrapping up, everyone was in high spirits. Rhea and Gautam had had their share of drinks but were composed. She had to drop him back to his aunt's house since he wasn't familiar with the city. Rhea wanted to go alone but Myra insisted on accompanying them. If Gautam was disappointed, he did a very good job of not showing it.

'You don't want to kiss him yet, Rhea. This is an arranged marriage meeting. He may be from the US but trust me, he will judge you if you kiss him. I'm coming along with you to drop him whether you like it or not. You will thank me for this.'

Rhea saw sense in Myra's words and they all headed to his aunt's house, which overlooked Juhu beach. Once they were outside the building, Gautam asked Rhea if she wanted to go for a walk on the beach.

Rhea's antennas went up! Firstly, it was late in the night and it wasn't safe to walk on the beach. Secondly, what did he expect Myra to do in the meanwhile? Thirdly, what were his intentions?

Rhea's high came down in an instant and she politely declined, citing safety reasons. Moreover, Myra's advice not to kiss him was also playing on her mind.

She didn't hear from Gautam after that. He was supposed to go to Delhi for a business meeting and then come back to Mumbai before he left for the US.

It was unbelievable and Rhea's hopes went back in the dumpster. Where was she going wrong? The question troubled her and kept her awake many nights.

15

Romance at Maasai Mara

2007
Mumbai

Matrimonial woes aside, things were going well for Rhea on the professional front. When her parents were not telling her about boys, she was travelling far and wide for work and pleasure alike.

Jaspal called her up before a holiday that she was taking to the exotic land of Maasai Mara with Neha, a friend from work. Thankfully, there had been a lull on the boys' front for some months and Rhea was happy to see the back of them.

'All set for your trip, *beta*?'

'Yes, Papa! All set. I'm flying out tomorrow night.'

'*Achha,* good! Riu, when you're back, there is this boy your mother wants you to meet. He's…'

'Papa, please don't give me any details right now. I want to enjoy my holiday. I haven't been able to take any time out from work the whole of last year. I don't want any boy's details playing on my mind while I'm away. Please let's discuss it once I'm back in 10 days' time.'

Rhea was looking forward to her trip and the wilderness of Maasai Mara, learning about the Great Migration, the Big Five, flora, fauna *et al.*

In the course of their holiday, they came across a group of backpacking Europeans who were staying in the same lodge as them. They were a group of five boys and three girls. After initial hellos and basic introductions, Neha quickly identified the two single boys in the group—Nathan Murray and Liam Fischer.

'Please don't let them be gay!' Neha whispered in Rhea's ear and they both laughed.

Neha was feeling flighty and she set off to chat up Nathan, leaving Rhea with no choice but to talk to the others in the group.

Before she knew it, Neha was back at her side, whispering, 'It's destiny. We were meant to meet. I like Nathan. I'm going to get to know him a little better. You hook up with Liam. He's single and totally heterosexual.'

She didn't know why she was feeling all shy and like a 16-year-old at the thought of talking to Liam. Both the single boys were Adonis-ly beautiful but there was something particularly mesmerising about Liam. She felt butterflies in her stomach when their eyes accidentally met.

Rhea secretly hoped that he would seek her out and she didn't have to wait for long. He was a charming man of 33 and she felt like a princess with all the attention he was showering on her.

After witnessing nature's miracles in all shapes and sizes at the Maasai Mara National Reserve, Rhea and Liam were holding hands and walking back to the Keekorok Lodge as if they had known each other forever. She turned to say goodbye to him in the lobby but he suggested she join him by the pool for an aperitif. She readily agreed.

Over a glass of Green Apple Martini, Liam and Rhea discussed the day's experiences and recalled their small special moments. Her favourite part was the beautiful sunset they had seen in vibrant red, orange and yellow hues while a pack of cheetahs lounged under a tree in front of them. Nature was magical and more so in silhouettes and Rhea felt blessed.

Liam was looking at her as if captivated by what she was saying. Rhea blushed but she was also feeling slightly bold after her first Martini. 'Why are you looking at me like that?'

'Do you know that your eyes dance and laugh when you talk about something you love?'

'Thank you.'

'You have a very expressive face, Rhea.'

Before she could say anything, Liam reached for her cheek and caressed it.

'You intrigue me, Rhea. I love saying your name over and over again. I've had such a wonderful day witnessing Africa in its full glory and it was that much more special because you were by my side.'

She could be a cynic and roll her eyes at his extra sweet words or she could be a romantic and go with the flow. The cynic was winning the mind war but the heart didn't want to break the magical spell. In the end, her heart won and she refrained from saying anything lest it jinx the moment.

She closed her eyes and for once stopped thinking and questioning what was happening. She wanted to live in the moment. Period.

'I cannot believe I'm acting like a teenager. I'm sorry but I've been bowled over by you, Rhea.'

'I like you too.'

They had another drink and lounged by the pool for another half an hour. Rhea didn't realise she had fallen asleep on his shoulder. She felt him waking her up gently. 'You look like an angel when you sleep. Peaceful and innocent.'

She smiled up at him and kissed him on his cheeks. 'You're really sweet, Liam.'

'Let me walk you to your room. I'm sure you're exhausted. We have a long day tomorrow too.'

They bid each other goodnight outside her room but not before he had kissed her forehead. She was touched by the gesture. 'Rhea, you should go inside now or I don't think I can trust myself to keep my hands off you.'

'Yes! I should go. Goodnight.'

She was happy-sad. Happy that he hadn't pushed her for more and sad for the same reason!

Neha wasn't in the room when Rhea walked in and she assumed she was with Nathan. 'Well, at least one of us is getting some action tonight!' Rhea said aloud in the empty room and snuggled into bed.

Ten minutes later, there was a knock on her door. Thinking it might be Neha, Rhea opened the door.

It was Liam and he looked almost apologetic. 'Nathan isn't opening the door to our room and I don't have the keys. I think he might be with Neha so I don't think it would be right of me to ask the Reception for a spare key. I didn't know where else to go.'

'Oh, okay! Come on in.'

Rhea felt rather self-conscious in her skimpy white nightwear, which was sprinkled with little red hearts. She didn't know what to do next so she waited for him to speak.

'Do you mind if I have a shower?'

'No! Not at all. Go ahead. There are some fresh towels in the bathroom.'

Rhea put the night lamp on and got back into bed, her heart beating fast in anticipation of what might happen next.

Her eyes were almost drooping shut when she felt the bed dip slightly as Liam got under the blanket. He smelt of white musk. It was one of her favourite fragrances. Almost intoxicated by the smell, Rhea pretended to sleep, praying frantically that her heartbeat didn't give her away.

Five minutes and he hadn't made any move to get closer. By now, Rhea was too exhausted after the day's travails to open her eyes. Her heartbeat was returning to normal and she was almost asleep when he called out her name softly.

She mumbled in her sleep.

'Come here, baby,' he said, ever so sweetly.

She moved closer to him without opening her eyes. This stranger had overwhelmed her. No words were necessary from either of them as he cocooned her in his arms and fell asleep.

Rhea slept like a baby. Liam hadn't laid a finger on her. He was mindful of the fact that she was tired and sleepy. What's more, here was a man who could keep his libido in check, a rarity!

She had another four days with him before their wonderful holiday would be over for good and this stranger would go back to his own world and she to hers.

'They say when you're having fun, time flies. I can't believe we're due to head back to the concrete jungle of Mumbai tomorrow. I wish we could stay a few more days,' said Rhea on the last night of their stay in Kenya. She didn't want to think about going back and the things that awaited her there. That part of her life was better off as a blind spot for the time being.

The girls bid tearful adieus to the group. Neha and Nathan had promised to keep in touch. Rhea hadn't wanted to keep in touch with Liam but he insisted on giving her his email address. 'One day when you do think of me, I don't want you to wonder where I may be. You can drop me a line and find out for yourself. I cannot force you to be in touch with me but I hope someday you will contact me. I will miss you, Rhea. You are a special girl.'

This is what movies are made of, thought Rhea. The few hours on the flight back home was all the luxury she would allow herself to think about Liam.

It was a sweet holiday romance. She would forget about it soon. She had to.

16

Compromise

When she got back to Mumbai, two important emails were waiting for her.

Bidding Neha goodbye, she hailed a cab outside the airport and waited until she was on her way home before she took out her BlackBerry.

Rohan Shroff! Her heart went pitter-patter on seeing his name. After four years of zero communication, he had decided to get back in touch: to send across his wedding invitation.

Rhea went momentarily numb. Her first love was getting married to someone else! Did he expect her to attend his wedding? She braced herself to read what he had to say.

From: RohanShroff <rohan666@gmail.com>

Date: Wed, 10Jun 2007 17:37:05 +0530

To: Rhea Khurrana<rhea.khurrana@gmail.com>

Subject: Wedding Invitation

Hii Rhea!

This email may come as a surprise but I couldn't help getting back in touch with you.

We have had so many glorious years together, fighting, arguing, screaming, scolding, caring and feeling for each other. We used to love the feeling of being together. We were hardly together physically but always there for each other in our hearts. We have literally grown together and seen the ups and downs of life. Right from the day your mother almost threatened me, to when I said nasty things to you, we have faced so many obstacles in our lives.

We have broken up twice (both because of my mistakes) and got back together (because you were supportive) and today it feels a bit weird to tell you that I am getting married. Yes, it is an arranged marriage. She is a sweet girl from Chandigarh.

I don't know how my life is going to be tomorrow but I want to tell you that you and I had something special and no one can take that away from us.

You may have felt bad when I didn't keep in touch after we broke up. But there was no way I could. Think practically, after so many years of togetherness, how could we be just friends?

I wanted to get in touch with you when I heard about your marriage but I just didn't know what to say. I'm sorry I didn't reach out to you then.

In the coming years, we may or may not choose to be in touch with each other. I may not even know where you are or what you are doing, but I will always respect you. I just want you to be happy.

Love,

Rohan

PS: The wedding is in Jalandhar. Please try to make it. I will feel good.

Rhea hadn't realised that there were tears streaming down her face. She didn't know why she was crying. He had to get married some day and it wasn't like she was still in love with him. He had not even crossed her mind recently. She angrily wiped away her tears but fresh ones trickled down. *So what if he's getting married?*

'I've moved on, he's moved on and it was a long time ago!' She tried telling herself that and then gave a short laugh. Her thoughts jumped to Liam. Maybe she was already missing the beautiful days she spent in Kenya with him and that's why she had such a strong reaction to Rohan's email. That would explain it. She was tempted to email Liam right away but stopped herself just in time.

There was another mail that needed her attention right now. This one was from her youngest sister, Geet, with an attachment about a boy's details and a photograph.

Curiosity made her want to glance at his photograph but it was taking way too long to open on her phone so she decided to look at it later. Besides, Rohan was on her mind. He had emailed her two days ago so she was a tad late in replying. There were a million things she wanted to tell him but decided she wouldn't. His email had messed up her mind. When she felt a little less hysterical, she called up Aditi.

'I don't understand what your big dilemma is. Politely decline his invitation and say you hope he has a good life ahead. Thank him for reaching out to you for old times' sake and that's it. End of chapter!'

'Yes! As simple as that! I'm glad I called you. Marriage seems to have made you pragmatic.'

They briefly caught up on each other's lives and then hung up. Rhea refrained from telling Aditi about Liam. She didn't feel like sharing him with anyone.

She quickly typed a brief reply to Rohan, congratulating him and saying exactly what Aditi had asked her to. She felt strangely at peace after sending it.

Rhea had forgotten about the email from Geet until Gurleen called her later that evening. After updating her about the holiday (minus Liam, of course), Rhea finally tucked into bed and checked out the profile of the guy her sister had sent.

Avinash Something was a Chartered Accountant by qualification and a professor by profession. One glance at his bio-data and Rhea knew he wasn't her type and moreover, she didn't want to settle in Patiala. His photograph was the only thing that left an impression.

Rhea was word-battling her mother the next morning and hoping to win.

'Where's the connection, Mumma? He's a professor and I'm in advertising. There is no match. What kind of a salary does a professor draw? I'm sure it's not even one-fourth of what I earn currently. I don't think there's any point in taking this forward.'

'Everything is not about money. He might be a good person, Rhea.'

'And what about me not wanting to settle down in Patiala? Why can't you find someone in Mumbai?'

'Have you been to Patiala lately? It's as good a city to live in as Mumbai. There has been so much development there in recent years and it's definitely less cluttered. Don't find excuses just for the sake of finding them, Rhea.'

'Pleeeeeeeease!'

'I hear Rohan is getting married. Don't you want to settle down too?' Gurleen was good at her game.

'How do you know?'

'Ruby Aunty told me. Word spreads fast in Jalandhar. But we're digressing. Avinash and his family have liked your profile and want us to come to Patiala over the weekend. I've asked your father to get our tickets booked.'

'You're basically telling me I have no say in this? Right? Everything's already decided. Do what you want. I'll talk to you later.'

Rhea lit a cigarette. Frustrated and angry, she had no idea how to deal with her mother. She was such a bully.

The weekend was four days away and she had a pile of work to catch up with before that. Rhea had a sudden urge to meet Tapan so she made a plan for that evening. He was always good for her when she was in a confused state of mind. Liam, Rohan and now Avinash; her plate was full, yet empty.

She tried to forget the conversation with her mother and went about her daily routine. She was so engrossed in her work that she lost track of time until Tapan called her.

'Don't tell me you're going to stand me up!'

'Shit! I didn't realise it's already 9 o'clock. I'll join you in 20 minutes.'

They had decided to meet at Otter's Club on Carter Road. Tapan was a member there and the booze was really cheap. He was sitting at the bar when she entered after signing herself in as his guest at the reception. 'How are you, my darling? You look radiant. The tan suits you!'

'Thanks, Taps! It would seem Africa agreed with me. Oh! Look, look, that's Randhir Kapoor sitting at the corner table. Who's that woman with him? Damn, I wish he had come with Bebo! Shall we take a picture with him? Please!'

Tapan slapped her on the wrist and said, 'Oh, you star-struck girl, grow up!'

Rhea made a sullen face but sat down nonetheless. The next moment, she forgot all about Randhir Kapoor. After catching up on some gossip from the advertising world, Tapan wanted to know what was playing on her mind.

'How do you know there's something bothering me?'

'I am your Pop when it comes to this so don't even try to pretend.'

'Well, what can I say? It's the same old story. I am fed up of the arranged marriage game my parents are making me play. It's very tedious to meet the boy, his parents, uncles, aunts, brothers, sisters, grandparents and God knows who else. I can't do it anymore but I have no choice. My parents expect me to join them in Patiala this weekend to meet yet another man.'

Rhea gave him the lowdown on everything she knew about Avinash. 'Go *na*! Why do you resist for the sake of resisting?'

'Oh! Please! You're beginning to sound like my mother!'

'Do you want to get married or not? Ask yourself that question. If the answer is "Yes" then you should be open to meeting guys and not resist just because they don't match the criteria on your list.'

'Of course I want to get married but to someone who has at least some things in common with me.'

'Isn't it unfair to reject this guy without meeting him and assuming you have nothing in common? Go and meet him, babe! What's there to lose?'

Rhea was loath to admit that Tapan was right. Hell! Even her mother had said the same thing. Maybe she was putting up a fight for no reason at all. Maybe it was time she let go of the bitter experience of the past.

'I guess I'm giving mixed signals to the universe!'

'The universe wants only the best for you. You are destined to live an abundant and fulfilling life, I can feel it. What's stopping you, Rhea? If you aren't happy with where you are right now, you are wrong to assume that it's your fate. Free yourself from fears like this. Remember, honey, there's always sunshine after the rain! *Capiche*?'

Rhea had tears in her eyes. 'Yes, I do, my wise old man! That is the sweetest thing anyone has ever said to me. Thank you!'

The next day, she booked her flight to Patiala after finding out her parents' travel schedule. Gurleen had not been able to hide the relief in her voice when Rhea told her she was booking her ticket.

Avinash's family, comprising his parents, younger brother and himself, lived in a cramped two-bedroom house. When Rhea reached his home, she was less than impressed. She couldn't visualise herself living here. Moreover, while his parents occupied one bedroom, Avinash and his brother shared the other. Rhea wondered what his brother would do once Avinash got married.

She forced herself to stop thinking on such lines and concentrated on the people around her.

Then came the inevitable 'get-to-know-each-other' part! Like she had done innumerable times before with other guys, she went into Avinash's room while both families chitchatted in the drawing room.

The more guys she met, the more she wondered about how two people were expected to make the life-altering decision of getting married after spending just a few minutes with each other. And to think that despite questioning it, she too had done just the same…not once but twice already!

While she wasn't able to comprehend it, almost the entire country was getting married in the same fashion with the exception of a select few. And they were all in a happy marriage…or at least in a long-lasting one. Weren't they? Maybe there was some secret formula to achieving the 'happily ever after' via the arranged marriage route. She wouldn't know without venturing forward.

Avinash seemed like a nice guy but then again, weren't they all? He was funny and smart in his own way. What surprised her, pleasantly, was the fact that he shared her apprehension about agreeing to marry someone after the very first meeting. 'That's a relief to hear. I share the same view as you. I think it's imperative that two people should try and get to know each other a little better before deciding whether they want to get married or not.'

Rhea felt comforted. At least now she won't have to give an answer to her parents immediately when they stepped out of his house.

They had plenty to talk about. She was keen to know what it was like to be a professor and teach college kids who were almost the same age. He wanted to find out what a normal day in the life of an advertising professional looked like. And for some time at least, Rhea forgot about the pressure looming over her head.

When her parents asked her what she thought about Avinash, she was non-committal. Gurleen was not satisfied and almost forced an answer out of her.

'Mumma, we've not decided anything. He suggested that we get to know each other a little better over the phone and then take a decision depending on how things go.'

'That's not bad. How much time does he want?'

Rhea sighed. Would Gurleen ever ask her how much time *she* wanted?

'A month or so,' Rhea now replied disinterestedly.

Over the next month, Rhea and Avinash stayed in touch over the phone. She had found a sweet friend but wasn't sure about marrying him. However, she didn't voice her thoughts aloud to anyone. For once, she wanted to give out the right signals to the universe. If this was meant to be, let it be. She had to get to know him thoroughly before taking a decision.

It was a good thing that at least she thought of him as a friend. Maybe a life-long relationship could be based on friendship. She tried not to think too much about his financial status. Anyway, didn't they say, *paisa toh haath ka maail hota hai*? Things could improve, right?

Rhea now knew for sure that she was earning more than him, which had the potential of becoming a sour point in their life if they got married. She didn't even know what kind of work opportunities there would be in Patiala for her if she decided to settle there. For the time being, she consciously stopped her mind from taking that line of thought forward.

Go with the flow, she kept telling herself.

She had grown to like Avinash, particularly the fact that he didn't smoke, drink or chew any of those disgusting *paan masalas*. She had been trying to quit smoking and maybe she could also try and give up alcohol after marriage.

At the end of one month, she was ready to say 'Yes' to this proposal if her parents asked her. She could live with him. She could be compromising on her lifestyle but that wasn't such a big issue in the larger scheme of things.

Just like that, without her knowledge, that much-loathed word, 'compromise', had quietly slithered into her life like a venomous serpent.

Avinash called her up after she had made up her mind. They chatted for a few minutes in general and then he turned her world upside down.

'I like you, Rhea, but only as a friend. We are very different people in terms of our aspirations and outlook towards life. I hope you find someone who will understand you in the way that I probably will never be able to.'

She was stunned. He was rejecting her when she had been ready to compromise with him. But Rhea couldn't hold it against him even if it hurt a little. She wished him a happy life.

'My God! It would have been another disaster in my life all over again! I convinced myself that he was the one for me. I think meeting Liam and then hearing about Rohan's wedding had left me feeling somewhat incomplete. But now I know, I'm not meant to make compromises. It just doesn't work like that,' Rhea was telling Neha at work the next day.

'The right one will come along if you have patience. Don't run after marriage, Rhea. Let it come to you.'

Neha's profound words were all Rhea needed to hear right now. They gave her hope. That day, she made a promise to herself: she would never compromise again when it came to choosing her partner. Never.

17

Inauspicious and Unlucky

2008-09
Mumbai

Most people come to have a fair idea of how they want their lives to pan out. Many chalk out the path they want to take and then work hard towards making it happen the way they had envisioned.

At 28, Rhea was one of the youngest boss ladies in the ad world but on the personal front she was a no-go. She harboured dreams of being married to a loving husband and having children. But that other side of green always evaded her.

Rhea remembered something Aadish had once told her: 'At one point, your life seems planned and organised and then suddenly, everything changes, leaving so many unanswered questions. We might stand at that junction of life and wonder what went wrong, an answer to which we may never find. I guess we have to learn to accept it and live with it forever.'

They were simple yet deep words and the message had stayed with Rhea. She had no answers as to why things went wrong with every relationship that she was hopeful about.

By now, a few of her younger cousins were already married. Rhea got the shock of her life when Jaspal informed her about a proposal that had come for Geet.

'Papa! She's only 25. It's too early for her to get married and she's the youngest amongst us. Times have changed. Let her study further if that's what she wants.'

Geet aspired to be a nutritionist and was doing a course in Nutrition and Dietetics from Pune University. Rhea couldn't see her getting married so early.

Preet, on the other hand, was the happy-go-lucky one. She had completed her Bachelors in Commerce from Fergusson College and was now working for an event management company in Pune. She still had to decide what she wanted to do in life and there was no pressure on her. Both of them were still young.

'We also think that we should wait another year or so. And besides, how can we get either of them married before you? I'm sure something will work out soon,' Jaspal reassured her.

Rhea felt the pressure mounting. If they found boys for the twins by next year, it would mean she *had* to get married before they did.

As they had grown older, Rhea had become closer to the twins. Gone were the days of their bratty teenage fights. She vaguely remembered Preet having a crush on a boy from Jalandhar a few years ago. However, Rhea had been so embroiled in her own life that she didn't even know if Preet was seeing anyone. On the other hand, she didn't think Geet could ever consider having such liaisons. She was single-mindedly focused on a career.

Rhea decided to speak to her sisters and dialled Geet. There was no answer so she tried calling Preet instead.

'Wassup, gorgeous? I hear there's a *rishta* for Geet!'

'Don't ask, Riu Di! It's so unreal. I'm now scared to tell Mom and Dad about Karan. Remember, I told you about him a year and a half ago.'

'Of course I remember him.'

'We have been seeing each other for a year and you know I've liked him forever. This *rishta* for Geet has come as a rude shock and made me realise that soon enough I may also be in the same situation. I think I should tell them before they decide to get me married to someone else.'

Rhea loved the clarity and courage that Preet had. What if she had also mustered up the courage to explain to her parents about Rohan? But this was not the time to delve into her life.

'You should tell them about him. Let me know if you want me to talk to them. I don't think they should have a problem. Karan is from a very nice family and from what you told me, he's doing well for himself.'

'That is not my concern. My main concern is Bittu Maharaj. If Lady Hitler decides to get our *kundali*s matched and for some reason they don't, then she is never going to allow me to get married to him.'

Preet and Geet had both been privy to the endless sessions Gurleen had with Bittu Maharaj to match Rhea's *kundali*s. It was not without reason that she was getting all worked up.

'Cross the bridge when you come to it, darling. First tell them about him and see how they react.'

Preet called her back the very next morning. 'Guess what, Di? I mustered up the courage to show Karan's photograph to Mom and Dad last night and told them about him. I think they liked him. They said they would meet his family soon and discuss how to take things forward. And I also wanted to tell you that Karan and I want to wait till you get married before making any announcements.'

Preet was a sweetheart. Rhea was pleased and relieved beyond measure that Gurleen had not made a hue and cry about Karan.

'I am so happy for you, baby sister. And thank you for being so considerate towards me but don't let my marriage come in the way of yours. Who knows when I will find someone? I don't want you both to wait.'

'Don't lose hope, di. It will happen soon for you too.'

Soon didn't even begin to describe it. Over the next year, neither did any proposals come for her, nor was there anyone in her circle of friends whom she was interested in. Rhea was relieved to be spared from the ordeal.

Meanwhile, Jaspal and Gurleen had met Karan's parents. Now that both families had given their consent, Karan's was keen on getting the pair engaged so that others wouldn't jabber unnecessarily. Indian society still had a long way to go before they stopped judging and taking to task two people who were in love but not wedded. Once a formal ceremony took place, tongues automatically stopped wagging.

Rhea knew that while her family was happy with Preet and Karan's pairing, they were a bit uncomfortable about the fact that Rhea, being the elder one, was still unmarried. They asked her time and again if it was okay that Preet was getting engaged before her. They didn't want to hurt her feelings.

Life had made Rhea strong. How could she let her feelings come in the way of her sister's happiness? Moreover, she was happy for Karan and Preet and it genuinely didn't bother her.

Another thought crossed Rhea's mind. Now that Gurleen was okay with the fact that one of her daughters had found her own life partner, maybe she should actively try dating some of the men who had earlier shown interest in her. Rhea had not really encouraged any of them because she didn't want her parents rejecting her choice.

Rhea gave Aditi the update.

'You know, Adu, by now I don't give a rat's ass about what the fucking society says. No one gets the benefit of the doubt anyway so who cares? Don't you agree?'

'Absolutely, babe! You shouldn't hassle yourself with what people say. They have a habit of making everyone's business their own! Chill and enjoy life!'

Preet and Karan were due to get engaged and married within a month's time. Gurleen wanted Rhea to come home and help with the preparations.

Rhea took three weeks' leave from work and went to Jalandhar. Memories from her own wedding preparations from a few years back rushed to her mind and she suddenly felt a wave of sadness engulfing her. She was quick to shrug it aside.

Life was chaotic in the two weeks leading up to the engagement and wedding ceremonies. There were a million things to take care of and Rhea took charge of almost everything that had to be done.

At night, she would lose herself in the numerous television series that she had on her computer's hard drive, ranging from *24*, *Boston Legal*, *Mad Men*, *Prison Break* to *How I Met Your Mother*. While the mornings zipped by in preparations, the nights were hers to watch TV shows and catch up with friends over Skype and GoogleTalk.

One night, while chatting with Megha, who was now working in Delhi, Rhea got a 'ping' from Rohit. It had been a few years since she had heard from him.

After saying 'bye' to Megha, Rhea started chatting with him. They talked about almost everything under the sun and caught up on each other's lives. Rhea had never before had any kind of personal conversation with him. He had a great sense of humour and Rhea was at the risk of waking up her family when she found herself laughing like a hyena at his wisecracks in the middle of the night.

It was almost 3 a.m. when they decided to log off. By the end of the conversation, Rhea and Rohit had added each other on BlackBerry Messenger.

She slept with a smile on her face for no particular reason at all. From that day on, Rhea and Rohit fell into a routine of BBM chats. Their day started with 'Good Mornings' and ended with 'Good Nights'.

A few days before Preet's engagement, guests started arriving from different parts of the country: aunts and uncles of all shapes and sizes were at their home, putting in their two cents' worth. Rhea was running helter-skelter the day they were due to go to Karan's house with the *shagun*. After finishing everything she had to do, she went to her room to change. Everyone else was ready. When she came out of her room after 15 minutes, all dressed up, she was stunned to see that her parents had already left. Rhea thought that maybe someone was waiting for her and went to check outside for a car. Finding no one there, she went back inside and asked one of her aunts why no one had called her before leaving.

'They must have forgotten in a hurry. The auspicious moment would have passed,' explained one of her father's cousins, Rinku.

'But *Buaji*, how can they forget me?' asked Rhea, still trying to digest what had happened.

'*Arrey*, Rhea, it's not like there's something major happening there. They will just exchange sweets and gifts and come back within an hour. You have a habit of making a big deal out of nothing. Stop whining and at least try to be happy for your sister who has found such a nice boy. And you should be happy if you can find someone even half as good. But God alone knows what life has in store for you.' This time it was the boisterous Twinkle *maasi*, a cousin of her mother's.

Rhea always knew her to be a bigmouth and a bully but her blunt and rude words cut right through her heart. Hurt and not wanting to create a scene, she turned to go back to her room without a retort.

While walking back, she suddenly stopped dead in her tracks when she overheard her aunts talking.

'How do we make her understand that a 29-year-old divorced and single elder sister of the bride mars an auspicious occasion with her presence alone? Gurleen should have told her in so many words not to go for the *shagun*,' she heard Twinkle tell Rinku.

Hearing those words marked the lowest juncture in Rhea's life and God knows she'd had her share of lows. She suddenly understood how Indian widows must have felt during the olden days when they were openly barred from participating in any celebrations.

Did they not want her to attend the engagement and wedding? Should she go back to Mumbai? But how could she not be a part of the most important day in her sister's life? Did they consider her unlucky? Did her parents also share the same thoughts? She immediately reprimanded herself for thinking like that. But why didn't they insist that she come along with them? When Geet had accompanied them to Karan's house, why not her? The answers to these questions were getting tougher and tougher.

Rhea didn't like the route her thoughts were taking. She didn't wait to hear Rinku's reply. The lesser she heard, the better and, for the time being, she had heard enough. She was not broken or so she kept telling herself until the tears fell unabated.

Rohit chose that very moment to ping her on BBM. She ignored it. When she didn't reply, he called her. It was not like Rohit to call her up immediately. He usually gave her some time to reply. She let his call go unanswered, being in no state to have a conversation with him.

Her mind was taking her to a dark and scary place. Rhea was on the verge of slipping into depression and began questioning life itself but then remembered the promise she had given her father some years back and pulled herself up.

This little wound would remain within her for a long time. There was no way that she could tell another soul what had happened without making her family look bad.

Rhea had a lot of things playing on her mind and before she knew it, she could hear some activity outside. Her parents must be back. She quickly changed into her home clothes, wiped off her tears, removed her make-up and stepped outside.

There was no way that she would be the cause of spoiling the merry environment. Now was not the time to make a big deal of what had happened. It would just be a keg in the wheel and mar the festive spirit at home. She would deal with her emotions privately, like she had done so far.

Society had its ways of breaking down a strong person. But she resolved that she wouldn't let anything break her. Not now! Not ever!

18

Mr. Special!

2010
Jalandhar

Had it not been for Rohit and his silly banter which made her laugh and forget her woes during the rest of her stay in Jalandhar, Rhea would have found it difficult to push that unpleasant incident off her mind. He knew something was bothering her but didn't push her to talk about it. She was relieved.

Rhea felt herself being drawn to him and she could tell that he felt something for her too. Despite having known each other for many years, they had never met in Mumbai except for the one time Rhea had gone to him while she was looking for a job. It was strange that they got back in touch while she was in Jalandhar, their hometown!

Rohit and Rhea. Together, their names had a nice ring. He had swiftly become a very special person in her life and Rhea smiled sheepishly in the mirror one morning just thinking about him. The very next moment, she straightened herself, her expression serious. She couldn't afford to throw caution to the wind! She felt an urgent need to talk to Aditi and ask for her advice.

'I'm glad you and Rohit are getting to know each other better but don't raise your hopes, Rhea. No use building castles in the air. I'm saying it for your own good. You've been hurt too many times in the past so tread carefully. If it's meant to happen, it will. Meanwhile, keep your eyes open so you don't get hurt.'

Sane, practical and logical advice! Even while her rational mind wanted to agree with Aditi and she knew it was exactly what she had called her to hear, the romantic in her had other ideas.

Rhea wanted somebody to tell her that falling in love was beautiful, that the magic was exhilarating despite the hurt it could be accompanied by. Regardless of the lows, it was a warm feeling to love and be loved. Alas! No one was telling her all this.

She hung up after promising Aditi that she would tread the Rohit path carefully.

Preet's wedding had gone off smoothly and Rhea was extremely happy for her sister and brother-in-law. She was due to leave for Mumbai in a couple of days and resume work. Her heart raced thinking about the impending meeting with Rohit.

2010-11
Mumbai

It had been almost four or five years since she had met him and that had been a brief and impersonal encounter. This time, it was going to be different. They had become friends…hell…who was she kidding? They were definitely a lot more than friends.

Hours before they were due to meet, Rhea was as nervous as a long-tailed cat in a room full of rocking chairs. She dressed casually but not too much, applied gloss but not lipstick, blow-dried her hair but was careful not to style it too much.

Rhea had vowed that she would not come across as too eager in front of him. She couldn't afford to show him how much he already meant to her.

Rohit was to come over right after work. They decided to meet at her house since it was close to his office. She was extremely fidgety after he called and told her that he was on his way.

They were so awkward with each other when they met that Rhea couldn't help but remember the scene from *Kuch Kuch Hota Hai* when Shah Rukh Khan and Kajol met for the first time after college at that 'stupid' summer camp!

Thanks to her over-imaginative filmy thoughts, her head was in the clouds more often than not. Just like 'Rahul' and 'Anjali', Rohit and Rhea didn't know whether to shake hands or hug or just say polite hellos to each other.

Telling her Bollywood mind to shut up, Rhea asked him inside and inquired whether he wanted water or juice or coffee.

'Coffee sounds good.'

'Super! I make the best coffee ever. You'll love it,' Rhea bragged. It was true; her coffee was truly praised by friends and family alike.

Rohit followed her into the kitchen and Rhea had butterflies in her stomach. She was beating the coffee in a mug near the kitchen sink when Rohit walked up to her from behind and put his arms around her waist. Her heart was racing.

'You're making me nervous.'

'Why, baby?' He said and kissed her cheeks, not letting go of her.

'Let me make the coffee, *na*. Don't distract me.'

He let go of her then and Rhea went about with the coffee. When it was ready and she tasted it, she almost spat it out. It was horrible and Rhea drained her cup in the sink.

'This is the worst coffee I have ever made or tasted and it's all because you were distracting me.'

But Rohit insisted he loved it even if his expressions told a completely different story. He finished it without complaining.

They chatted in general about random things and when the conversation dried up, they would just look into each other's eyes and smile.

After an hour or so, Rohit decided to leave and she went to see him off. As she reached for the doorknob, Rohit turned her towards him and hugged her tight. Heart pounding, she hugged him back. She felt a deep sense of belonging.

Play!
Have I told you lately that I love you
Have I told you there's no one else above you
Fill my heart with gladness
Take away all my sadness
Ease my troubles that's what you do

'I love you.' Rhea said, lost in his arms as she hummed the song in her mind, aware of nothing else but him until it struck her suddenly that she had said the words out aloud.

Shit! Shit! Shit!

She knew she had messed up. Rhea cringed, shutting her eyes tightly, wishing she could turn back time…all this while she was still in his arms.

'And I've loved you even before Rohan happened to you.'

She couldn't be sure if Rohit had actually said that. *Didn't he have a girlfriend back in school? How could he have loved her then?* She had to stop the questions from coming into her mind. She tuned back to the present and looked up at him.

'What did you just say?'

'You heard me.'

'I'm not sure if I heard right.'

'I said I've loved you before you and Rohan started seeing each other in school. I think I fell in love with you when I first saw you outside that tuition class when Shaila casually introduced us.'

'I don't believe you. Why didn't you say anything to me till now?'

'The opportunity never came up.'

He had loved her since then and had never said a word? It was preposterous but then again, maybe not. The fear of rejection and the woes that came with unrequited love could make many falter in their footsteps.

Rhea remembered the few times that Rohit had tried to make conversation with her over chat the last few years. But she hadn't given it much of a thought as there were other things on her mind.

At that time, she had not really been open to pursuing a conversation with him in the first place. If she had, who knows, things might have been different today.

There was no point delving into the past. The universe's bigger game had brought them together now and not then! She wanted this relationship to last over the long haul and she knew she had to be extra careful while walking down that road. Rhea was not a fan of heartbreaks. Life had thrown enough lemons at her. She was now ready to put some vodka in the mix and enjoy herself.

Rohit and Rhea made time for each other during the weekends, as they were both busy with their jobs through the week. They caught up on movies and plays together, went out for dinners and did the usual things that couples did.

'Move in with me.' Rohit sprang a surprise on her one day.

'Move in? My parents will never allow it, baby.'

'Let's not tell them for the time being.'

'I can't hide such a big thing from my family. To lie about it doesn't seem right.'

'Think about it. It will be so convenient. We won't be restricted to meeting only on weekends. I'd love to come back home to you every night and wake up next to you every morning.'

When he said things like that, she was tempted. She suggested a possible solution.

'How about we confide in our parents about our relationship and then tell them that we want to move in together?'

'It's way too soon for us to tell our parents, Rhea.'

'Oh! It's not too soon for us to move in together but it is too soon to tell our parents about us?'

She could feel a fight brewing up. If it did, this would be their first.

'Don't misunderstand me, Rhea. We've hardly been with each other for six months. It is too soon to get our parents involved. Telling them right now will raise their expectations and I don't want any pressure building up on that front.'

'Well, then you should know that I won't move in with you without informing my parents. Since it's a Catch 22 situation, we might as well drop the topic.'

And the chapter was closed. Something kept nagging Rhea about this conversation. She chose to tackle it later.

There was a lot of pressure on the work front. She was due to leave in a week's time for the Cannes Lions International Festival of Creativity with the bossman, Sagar Mittal, Neha and another colleague. She was looking forward to seven days of networking coupled with generous doses of fun and frolic and, of course, the awards.

Rhea also thought this break would do her relationship with Rohit some good. The strain had somehow not left her ever since the 'moving in' conversation. However, Rohit was either least affected by it or he did a good job of hiding it.

Things miraculously changed when she was in Cannes and Rhea saw not one but many beacons of hope and sunshine. Rohit was the perfect boyfriend. He called her up every day while she was away, sometimes not once but twice. They also exchanged BBMs frequently through the day.

She was shopping one evening with Neha in the incandescent streets of Cannes when Rohit called her.

'Hi, baby! Wassup!'

After hearing what he had to say, Rhea's pitch went from soft to shrill in a matter of seconds.

'Are you serious? Really? I don't believe you. What happened that you're suddenly telling me this? Yes! Yes! Okay, I will. I love you too!'

Neha was looking at her expectantly with life-size questions in her eyes.

'He wants me to meet his parents when I return. Can you believe it? Just a week ago when he asked me to move in with him, it was too soon to get our parents involved and suddenly it isn't anymore.'

'That is great. Don't question it too much. More often than not, guys are confused about taking a relationship to the next level. If this one is asking you to meet his parents, it means he's serious.'

'Yes! I know. We might even be doing a *roka* once I get back to Mumbai.'

'Wow! That is wonderful news! I'm so happy for you.'

Rhea couldn't wait to tell her father about this new development in her life. After Preet's wedding, Jaspal really wanted her to settle down too. He even told her once that if there was anyone she liked, she shouldn't hesitate to tell him about it. Now was the time to do just that!

She immediately called him up and apprised him of the latest development in her life. His joy knew no bounds.

During her last two days in Cannes, Rhea was so happy that she just couldn't wait to get back to Mumbai. Rohit had even made her speak to his parents over the phone one evening. Ten minutes into the conversation and they had become 'Ma' and 'Pa' for her instead of 'Aunty' and 'Uncle'.

True happiness was finally knocking on her door after years of drudgery in the love department and she was ready to welcome it with open arms. It seemed as if life was perfect.

Rohit was coming to pick her up from the airport. When she called him after her flight landed, his voice sounded hoarse. He was sick and couldn't make it.

'Oh, poor baby! Don't worry. I'll take a cab and come to your place. Should I pick up some chicken soup for you on the way?'

'No! I've just taken some medicines and it's making me drowsy. By the time you get here, I will be asleep. Let's meet tomorrow.'

Rhea didn't know why it angered her to hear him say that. After saying a curt 'Okay,' she hung up.

'Never expect anything from anyone. They are bound to let you down. I think I've learnt my lesson.'

Exasperated as ever, Rhea was fuming as she and Neha shared a cab.

'He may be genuinely unwell. Why are you so angry?'

'I guess I'm disappointed.'

'Meet him tomorrow.'

But that 'tomorrow' never came. Rhea kept making plans to catch up with Rohit and he kept making excuses. Meanwhile, she was talking to his parents almost every week and they couldn't wait to meet her.

Just like that, four months had passed since she had come back from Cannes and all she heard from Rohit were excuses. She was fed up now.

Fuck him! If he didn't want to meet her, he could go to hell. Rhea stopped calling him and his parents.

One rainy evening in July, she was sitting at a cosy bar in Bandra with Neha and a few other colleagues after a meeting when she got a call from Rohit. Why was he calling her?

She let the call go unanswered. Immediately after that, she got a call from Surinder Uncle, who inquired whether she was safe as there had been bomb blasts in Zaveri Bazaar, Opera House and Dadar.

Now Rhea knew why Rohit had called but she was in no mood whatsoever to entertain his call or even give him the assurance that she was alright. He called a couple of more times and she didn't answer.

'Who is that calling you again and again and why aren't you answering? Whoever it is might be worried for your safety,' said a concerned Neha.

'It's Rohit. Let him suffer and think I've died in the bomb blasts. Serves him right.'

Just as the words were out of her mouth, Rhea winced at how bitter she sounded. She finally messaged him back.

'I'm safe. Nothing to worry about. Hope you're okay.'

She was curt and to the point. That was it. After that, he made no effort to reach out to her over the coming days.

Rhea's heart was stuck on him but her ego didn't allow her to make any more effort. That weekend she went with Neha for *Zindagi Na Milegi Dobara*, which had released in theatres despite the tense situation in the city. To distract herself from thinking about him, Rhea went for the movie again with Myra the next day. It was a magical movie about friends, life and love.

She felt the need to be around her friends. A few weeks later, Neha had got a promotion at work and the two of them decided to go for a night on the town without any men.

'I've not told you this before and I'm only telling you now because I'm drunk but I spent ₹2 lakh on buying a fucking Rolex for Rohit when we were in Cannes! It was an impulsive buy! I know he loves watches. All I wanted was to see the happiness on his face when I gave it to him. Now there won't be any such moment. I don't know what went wrong. I never do! Is a little bit of love too much to ask for? Tell me… is it?'

Rhea wanted to drink and drown in her sorrow and Neha provided the much-needed shoulder to cry on.

'He got cold feet, Rhea. It's as simple as that. While you were away, he must have really missed you. People commit to a lot of things when they are emotional. When those emotions pass, reality strikes and they backtrack.'

Neha's words were making a lot of sense. In her drunkenness, Rhea recited the poem from her now favourite *Zindagi Na Milegi Dobara* movie, which she had seen five times already.

Jab jab dard ka baadal chaya
Jab ghum ka saya lehraya
Jab aansoo palkon tak aaya
Jab yeh tanha dil ghabraya
Humne dil ko yeh samjhaya
Dil aakhir tu kyun rota hai
Duniya mein yunhi hota hai

'It's my favourite movie. And life's a bitch, Neha! Let's drink to that! Cheers!'

The deep sense of hurt behind those lines was not lost on Neha.

Rhea spent the night at Neha's place. Life was beginning to amuse her. How silly people were to play games with each other at the risk of hurting someone or getting hurt themselves. Was it even worth it?

Headphones plugged in her ears; she played a song on repeat until her iPod battery drained out.

Play!
Touch me and I will follow
In your afterglow
Heal me from all this sorrow
As I let you go…
I will find my way
When I see your eyes
Now I'm living in your afterglow…

19

Girlfriend, Not Wife!

Rhea's little sister was going to be a mother soon. Preet was pregnant with her first baby and everyone in the family was overjoyed. Rhea decided to surprise them all with a visit to Jalandhar.

One evening, while having a drink with her father, he asked her about Rohit.

'There's nothing left of the relationship, Papa. I've not heard from him in almost six months now.'

A hundred and fifty three days, to be precise. She had been counting even when she didn't want to. While in Mumbai, it was easier not to think about him with her busy work schedule and social life; Jalandhar was a different story altogether. Her mind inevitably drifted to the happy days that Rohit and she had shared early on in their relationship.

Rhea was thinking about him so much these days that it was almost uncanny when she saw an email from him. It was as if the universe had conspired to make it happen for her.

Agar kisi cheez ko sacche dil se chaho toh puri kaynaat usse tumse milane mein lag jaati hai.

There was no limit to Hindi films influencing her thinking. She put aside the drama from *Om Shanti Om* and read what he had written.

From: Rohit Khanna <rohitkhanna79@gmail.com>
Date: Sun, 25 Dec 2011 10:39:11 +0530
To: Rhea <rhea.khurrana@gmail.com>

Subject: hi

Hi there,

I hope you are well. Been trying to get in touch with you for a while. Tried your number a couple of times but it didn't work. Could we chat for a bit? It would be nice if you could let me know. I am not sure if you have my number: it's +91-2291985198. Do let me know if it's okay for you to talk. Even if you choose not to, I request you to let me know.

Best,

Rohit

'Papa! Look at this email. I don't think I'm going to reply. I shouldn't, right?'

'Don't let your ego come in the way. Everyone deserves a second chance. At least find out what he wants to say. Think of it as a Christmas gift.'

'From your Santa Singh, no doubt! You're such a softie. Let me think about it.'

But reply she did, although a few hours later.

From: Rhea Khurrana <rhea.khurrana@gmail.com>
Date: Sun, 25 Dec 2011 14:34:11 +0530
To: Rohit Khanna <rohitkhanna79@gmail.com>
Subject: Re: hi

My number's changed. What do you want to talk about?

From: Rohit Khanna <rohitkhanna79@gmail.com>
Date: Sun, 25 Dec 2011 14:46:32 +0530
To: Rhea <rhea.khurrana@gmail.com>
Subject: Re: hi

About you and me.

From: Rhea Khurrana <rhea.khurrana@gmail.com>
Date: Sun, 25 Dec 2011 15:18:17 +0530
To: Rohit Khanna <rohitkhanna79@gmail.com>
Subject: Re: hi

Give me one good reason why I should talk to you about you and me!

From: Rohit Khanna <rohitkhanna79@gmail.com>
Date: Sun, 25 Dec 2011 15:33:34 +0530
To: Rhea <rhea.khurrana@gmail.com>
Subject: Re: hi

'Cause if it's about you and me it has to be you and me talking about it.

Very smart! That didn't warrant a response. Rhea decided not to reply.

From: Rohit Khanna <rohitkhanna79@gmail.com>
Date: Sun, 25 Dec 2011 16:49:04 +0530
To: Rhea <rhea.khurrana@gmail.com>
Subject: Re: hi

Say something!

Damn! Might as well get it over with. She thought aloud and typed her response.

From: Rhea Khurrana <rhea.khurrana@gmail.com>
Date: Sun, 25 Dec 2011 17:14:11 +0530
To: Rohit Khanna <rohitkhanna79@gmail.com>
Subject: Re: hi

Call me at 9.30 p.m. #988-158-1114

It was 8.30 p.m. and Rhea was strolling restlessly around the house. He would call her in another hour.

At 8.45 p.m., there was an SMS from him.

'In the hospital. Won't be able to call at 9.30.'

'No problem. Hope all's well.'

'Brother's son in ICU. Later.'

For a moment, Rhea thought he was giving her excuses yet again. Maybe he changed his mind since they had exchanged emails. But no one made stories about their family being in the ICU. Rhea didn't like the doubting person she had turned into. She had to give him the benefit of the doubt and believe what he said.

Rohit did message her again later in the night updating him about his nephew's condition. The doctors had diagnosed him with meningitis and suggested keeping him under observation for a week.

She knew he was worried and she also knew that her silly heart was willing to forgive him for the pain he had caused her.

That was her first mistake.

Rohit and Rhea got back together after having a few superfluous discussions on what went wrong in their relationship earlier. She didn't stress enough on addressing the core issue of commitment and chose to slide it under the carpet.

That was her second mistake.

By the time Rhea got back to Mumbai after spending some quality time with her family, she was hoping to get off to a fresh start. He was preoccupied with work and his nephew's health. While she was supportive of him, she was also getting restless. This was not the 'getting back together' that she had envisioned. Rohit wasn't making enough effort to woo her back and she couldn't bear the fact that the same thing was happening to her all over again.

An old friend from school, Sudipto Sarkar, pinged her on Facebook one night. He gauged her melancholic mood from their chat and asked if something was bothering her.

Rhea found strange solace in pouring her heart out to someone relatively far away and disconnected from her life. She, however, chose not to mention Rohit's name. They were all from the same town and she didn't want anyone judging him.

Sudipto's views brought in the man's perspective.

'Try and give him a dose of his own medicine. Don't take his calls sometimes. Make him wonder a bit. Put in some subtle hints that you prefer if he called more than once a day. Don't show sarcasm or anger. That, in a way, gives a man pleasure. One thing I've learnt is to be a gentleman and sometimes we Indians are anything but. We take pleasure in a woman's agony, not realising how much women appreciate chivalry.'

Rhea was totally taken in by his words. She wondered that when there were so many people giving her sane advice, why was it difficult for her to follow any of it?

'From what I've understood, you have to know that he's okay to have you as his "girlfriend" but not prepared to look at you as a "wife". He thought he was when he made you speak to his parents but then he probably realised his freedom meant more to him than you ever did. Something must have triggered off his thoughts or feelings when he got back in touch with you again, and then those feelings passed. He seems very fickle. Don't waste your time on him. You deserve better.'

Rhea faced up to the fact that it wasn't her ego that was stopping her from calling him or texting him; it was his unresponsiveness that cut like a knife through her heart. This made her stop taking any more initiative in this relationship. It seemed like the tables had turned and now she was the one facing the fear of rejection.

But she loved him. She was lucky to fall in love for the second time in her life and couldn't give up on it without making one last ditch effort to salvage what they had.

It was time to write her version of the 'Dear John' letter and then, depending on his response, she would move ahead either with or without him.

Hi R,

Since I haven't been able to communicate with you, I'm writing this to tell you what I feel because it bothers me to keep things in my heart.

I've been in Mumbai for two weeks and we've hardly even met! I don't see any initiative from you to call me up, message me or make a plan to catch up.

I will make the effort because I care for you but I won't do much if it's not reciprocated. I did make an effort and spoke to your Mom after you told her I was back in town. But if I don't hear from you for days together, why am I even doing that? On a day-to-day basis, I don't receive any kind of communication from you, forget love or attention! It's a basic want. It's a basic need. It makes me think about what I'm doing and if I'm so stupid that I'm making the same mistake for the second time with the same guy??!! I'd definitely have to be stupid!

You keep talking about problems in your life due to which you don't have the time or the inclination to connect with me. Maybe it's time for you to introspect on what you want from life. Maybe you don't even want or need me. Figure out your priorities. Work, friends, family, love. That's all there is to life, isn't it?

Whenever we've had an issue, you hide behind your problems. They'll always be there... that's life! It challenges and tests you everyday. You have to be in control of situations and not let situations control you. Name one person who doesn't have problems in life?

Even I have problems just like you and everyone else. But I will still smile when you call me, when you message me and when you meet me. I will still smile when I meet my friends and family because these things make me happy and my problems seem dwarfed, for that moment at least. I try not to let them get the better of me. Yes, I have my lows but I give them only as much importance as they deserve, not more, because I believe this too shall pass!

Shit happens in life. What's important is that you keep your head above it at all times.

Figure out what you want but don't take forever to do that! Start with the small things. They'll automatically pave the way for the bigger ones.

We were naïve to even think about our roka *last year. Right now I'm not even thinking of getting married to you because it would not work. And I know that word scares you to death! I'm unsure too about how it would be. Right now I'm just trying to give 'us' a shot. Maybe we'll hit the bull's eye. Maybe we'll be way off the mark. But you won't know without trying.*

I have some basic expectations from this relationship and they're not being met. I'm sure you have some expectations from me too, which I may not hold up to. We're not teenagers anymore and shouldn't waste precious time in thoughts, we should communicate and figure this out.

If a relationship with me doesn't make you happy and excited enough to want to meet me and talk and just be together then don't push it. But you have to be frank and tell me so I won't expect anything from you.

I guess I've said what I wanted to! If you want to give this a shot, we have to work on it together without letting our egos get in the way. If not, then I wish you happiness always, wherever you are and in whatever you do.

Rhea.

She re-read the email twice after finishing it. Satisfied, she finally hit the 'send' button and waited for a response. In the age of iPhones and BlackBerrys, one didn't have to wonder if the person had read your message. Of course they had.

After she sent it, Rhea's anxiety levels increased by the hour. She decided to distract herself. By the end of the day, she hadn't received a response from him and she knew she had made a huge mistake. He didn't care about her.

Silent tears rolled down her cheeks onto the pillow. Slowly, they turned into violent sobs until she fell asleep, physically and mentally drained by the outburst.

The next morning, there was still no word from Rohit and she wanted to disappear. She called up Myra and they both decided to scoot off to Goa. Myra understood Rhea's need to get away and booked them into Zuri White Sands Resort at Varca Beach in south Goa.

Goa was just what she needed. It was off-season so the place wasn't crowded and that suited the girls perfectly. They spent the entire afternoon in the swimming pool, which had an adjoining bar. It was perfect.

They hired a bike and decided to explore the terrain. Just then, it began to rain and Rhea had the time of her life. The beaches, the earthy smell from the rain, the greenery, the sunset…life was beautiful again and before she knew it, their three-day holiday was about to end.

She and Myra decided to spend their last evening like mermaids in the pool with cocktails galore for company!

Rhea's phone pinged. Rohit was BBM-ing her! It had been almost five days since she had sent him the mail and now she didn't want to know what he was saying. After five days of heartache, she had made herself immune, telling herself that he was just not worth her tears.

She decided not to read it but then, music intervened. The DJ decided to play one of Rohit's favourite songs by Pink Floyd at that very moment. Rhea particularly liked the last few lines… Was it a sign?

Play!
How I wish, how I wish you were here
We're just two lost souls swimming in a fish bowl, year after year
Running over the same old ground
What have we found?
The same old fears
Wish you were here!

She snapped back to the issue at hand. There was no point procrastinating. Rhea decided to read his message and get over with it once and for all.

Hi, sorry haven't been able to communicate to your mail. I do have to confess that it was hard-hitting and made all the relevant points. And I'll be honest, I didn't know how to respond. Have been thinking about it since the day I read it. I don't know the answers myself. But I know what's keeping me back. I'm scared of commitment. All your points are valid and I respect that, I feel for you as well but then I hesitate the moment seriousness creeps in. Don't know what more to say to explain myself.

Bloody creep! As if seriousness was a serpent that crept in! After that moment of anger, Rhea felt nothing and didn't bother replying. This would be the end of the Rohit chapter in her life.

After reading his message out loud to Myra, Rhea said, 'You know, Myra, when people don't think twice before trampling all over your heart; it becomes difficult to remember what you saw in them in the first place. It's not easy to give yourself the answers because no matter what, you can never lie to yourself. And trust me you just don't want to accept the fact that your judgment went so wrong. It's a tricky place to be in.'

'You tried, sweetheart. Sometimes you have to take a step back and distance yourself. If the other person cares, they will take notice and make an effort to bridge the distance. If they don't, then you know that it wasn't worth it in the first place. You lay your heart open for him and he chose to look the other way. Don't beat yourself up over the fact that it didn't work, be glad that you learnt something.'

Yes! Myra was right. Here was a 34-year-old who was afraid of commitment and scared to take the plunge, petrified of losing his bachelorhood, his freedom. Rhea was glad to see his back. Her heart would have to unlearn the art of loving him.

Rhea was lost in her thoughts when suddenly she burst out laughing and at the same time couldn't help a solitary tear from escaping her eyes...

This DJ at Zuri had psychic powers; as soon as she heard MJ's voice, she was even more certain.

Play!
One day in your life
You'll remember a place
Someone touching your face
You'll come back and you'll look around, you'll...
One day in your life
You'll remember the love you found here
You'll remember me somehow
Though you don't need me now
I will stay in your heart
And when things fall apart
You'll remember one day...

'Myra, Rohit will remember me one day but by then it would be too late.'

20

It's Not Over Till the Fat Lady Sings!

2012
Mumbai

Fate had been playing cruel games with Rhea for years and she was finally ready to say, 'Game On.'

No more tears and no more chasing after love.

'Don't be dependent on others for your happiness. You have to find your happiness from within, Rhea,' Tapan had once told her. Now she was going to do just that.

Over the years, the two boys with whom she had fallen truly in love with had treated her shoddily, causing irrevocable damage to her heart, her feelings and her dreams.

Over the years, her mother had placated and given Wahe Guru the responsibility of finding a 'nice' husband for her eldest daughter.

Over the years, Aditi had moved to Singapore with Vivaan and was now a mother of two angelic girls.

Over the years, Gurleen had found a nice Punjabi *munda* from Amritsar for Geet and Preet had given birth to adorable twin boys.

Over the years, Rhea had grown more and more adamant that getting married and having a companion for life was important but without any compromises.

By now, Neha had moved to another agency but they had kept in touch. She had recently started seeing Mayank, who worked with her. Neha kept encouraging her to start dating but Rhea was not in the mood to meet new men. However, Neha was relentless.

'Wassup, soulmate!' said Rhea when Neha called her up one evening.

'Wassup, honey! Listen, there's this guy I want you to meet.'

'Really now! Hardly has my mother stopped playing matchmaker when you, of all people, make it your hobby.'

'Shut up and don't be so closed towards new things in life. It's high time you stop your "Rohit *rona*" and start dating other men.'

'That's unfair. You know I'm over him.'

'Sure! And I was born yesterday!'

'Okay, whatever! So who is he?'

'His name is Armaan Agnihotri and he is Mayank's best friend from Doon School. He recently moved to Mumbai from Delhi and is the Vice President at PwC.'

'Are you expecting me to go on a blind date with him? And let me tell you that if you are, then I'm refusing right away. This is not open for negotiations.'

'Oh God, you're so closed and difficult. Can you at least hear me out? Mayank is throwing a Christmas party at his place this weekend and it's also going be a welcome party for Armaan. I'm going to introduce you guys there so you better not come in jeans and a tee. You have been warned. Go the spa if you have to and dress to kill!'

'Don't put pressure on me. I wish you hadn't told me. It would have been so much better if you had just made me meet him at the party.'

'Yeah! Yeah! Okay, bye! Remember, dress to kill and wear the Ruby Woo, you know, just to add drama.'

'Bitch! Hang up now! I'll see you on Saturday.'

Saturday night came way too soon and Rhea was nervous. For the nth time, she wished Neha hadn't mentioned Armaan beforehand. It added to the pressure of socialising, especially when you knew the agenda behind it.

If ever she had come across a person with the gift of the gab, it was Armaan. He was intelligent and witty and a player. Rhea could smell it off him and she warned herself not to get taken in by his smooth talk. She didn't want to come across as too friendly so she flitted from one group to the other at the party.

'He's been eyeing you all evening, Rhea. You look delectable in this navy blue dress. Can you please let your guard down for once? Drink up if you have to. He is a nice guy and it's obvious that you're avoiding him,' whispered Neha in her ear around midnight, her voice laced with displeasure.

'Don't be silly, Neha. I'm not avoiding him.'

'Whatever, babes! It's your call.'

'Don't whatever me now and spoil your mood. I will go and speak to him in some time.'

'That's my girl.'

Armaan was by her side before Rhea could go up and talk to him. Coming really close, he whispered conspiratorially in her ear. 'I see you've been avoiding me!'

Rhea was taken aback by his proximity and directness. Her antennae immediately went up. She had to think on her feet.

'Oh! Have I now? I am so sorry! I'll have to reprimand my subconscious mind for that,' said Rhea, in mock innocence.

'Oh! She has horns!' He laughed whole-heartedly.

'They help me balance my halo,' said Rhea with a straight face.

As if it wasn't enough that he was a hot and charming man, he had a deep, sexy laugh, which reverberated across the room. She caught many heads turning in his direction.

The fact that she had made this alpha male laugh gave her a thrill. The ice seemed to have broken between them and Rhea didn't realise how time flew. They laughed a lot and engaged in harmless flirting until he made a move on her.

He put his hand around her waist and before she knew it, nibbled on her ear. Rhea was stunned out of her wits by his audacity.

'Hey! Get your hands off me, Armaan. This is not cool. Are you drunk?'

'Of course not! Do I look drunk to you? Don't be such a prude, Rhea! I know you want me and you know I want you. Why waste time on social niceties?'

'If you weren't Mayank's best buddy, I would have slapped you right across your face for saying that.'

With that, she turned and walked right out of the party. She was shaking from head to toe and thought it better to leave without telling Neha. She didn't want to spoil the party.

That bastard! How dare he!

Half an hour later, Neha was frantically calling her but she was in no mood to talk to anyone. When Rhea called her back the next morning, Neha profusely apologised for Armaan's behaviour and blamed it on alcohol.

'Babes! One could study in the best of schools and work in the best of companies but if you don't know how to respect a woman, what use is all that? What he did and said is not nice, alcohol or no alcohol. Beyond this, I don't see the point in talking about it.'

Armaan took her number from Neha and sent her an apology message but she was in no mood to forgive. She put the incident behind her without replying and moved on.

Work was going great guns and Rhea got an opportunity to shift base to Hong Kong as the business head of the new office. She was seriously contemplating taking it up since it would broaden her horizons. A change of scene at this time would do her good.

The paperwork would take approximately three weeks and then Rhea could start a new life. The timing couldn't have been more perfect.

Two days before she was to leave for Hong Kong, Preet emailed her the details and photograph of a 39-year-old divorced Punjabi guy from New Jersey.

It was time to call Preet.

'Hi, lil' sister. I got your email and that's why I'm calling. He's nice-looking but isn't 39 a little too old? How do you know him? Have you told Mumma about it? Why did he divorce his wife? How many years was he married? Does he have kids?'

Rhea had infinite questions and the information Preet provided about Rakesh Kapoor left her feeling confused. Rhea was somewhat iffy about talking to him immediately but she didn't want to disappoint Preet. Rakesh would be calling her soon.

In her packing frenzy, Rhea had all but forgotten about him until her phone rang when she was killing time at the airport after the security check-in. What started off as a nice conversation became more and more cumbersome as the minutes ticked by. She almost saw it as divine intervention when the call to board her flight was announced.

On the long flight to Hong Kong, Rhea recounted her conversation with Rakesh.

He was a divorced 39-year-old who had been married to his high school sweetheart for eight years. She was an American and they had been seeing each other for three years before they got married. While culturally they both were totally different, love made them overlook their differences. However, what Rakesh couldn't put under the carpet was Mellissa's decision to not have children. She was an ambitious girl who wanted to touch newer heights in her career and saw children as a hindrance in attaining this goal.

After his divorce to Mellissa, Rakesh was looking at settling down but, once bitten twice shy, hence he was cautious. 'This time when I get married, I want to make sure our expectations about family life, lifestyle, upbringing and chemistry match,' he told Rhea over the phone.

He took it upon himself to prepare her for the American winter since, in his experience, Indians tended to get depressed during the winter in the US. To Rhea's horror, he went on to explain the four seasons—Spring, Summer, Winter and Fall—with a special emphasis on how dull, dreary and depressing winter was. Rhea felt as if she had been transported to her geography class in school where Mrs. Rana once taught them about the different seasons across different hemispheres.

Rhea's mind switched off until she heard him asking her a question. What followed were multiple queries ranging from her likes and dislikes, her 'interest' in household chores to her views on religion (by now she knew that it would be considered sacrilegious if 'they' didn't ask about her religious views). He wanted to know all about her preferences and capabilities. By the time she hung up, she felt as if she had just been interviewed for the position of a maid.

Rhea had half a mind to say, *Yes, I can wash clothes, I can cook, just don't expect gourmet fare. I can clean the house and utensils and I am a pretty responsible person. Oh and yes, I do love children. Shall we talk salary now?* But she had held her tongue.

She had no idea when she dozed off and the next thing she knew, the stewardess was gently waking her up for breakfast. Rhea sighed and pushed Rakesh to the back of her mind as if he had been part of a dream. She had much to look forward to in

Hong Kong. A whole new life was waiting for her and she was all set for a new beginning.

But if Rhea thought her life in Hong Kong would be a cakewalk, she was mistaken. Hardly had three months gone by when the pressures of a new country, workplace and the challenges that came with it started overwhelming her. To begin with, Rhea was somewhat shocked when she found out that every single person in her office was much older than her. To add to that, they were all married. She felt like she'd been transported into a traditional old-school office rather than a hip and buzzing advertising agency. It was a bit odd that there were no young hires at the agency. Maybe she could take the matter up with the bosses. As head of the Hong Kong branch, it was a daunting task for Rhea to bring out the pep in her drab colleagues.

With absolutely no one her age to hang around with, Rhea ended up going home alone every night after work. When she did try and make plans with the married couples, she felt thoroughly left out and stuck out like a sore thumb in their all-comfy world.

There was no one in Hong Kong she could turn to or fall back on. A few months into her zestless and dismal routine, Rhea felt a sense of dread engulfing her.

'Myra! Does your schedule allow you to take a break and come to Hong Kong? I'm not sure what is wrong but I feel my heart pounding heavily everyday. It's a very uneasy feeling. I get palpitations as soon as I wake up and there's a sense of breathlessness. I don't know what I'm scared of but there's always an awful feeling in the pit of my stomach. I don't know if you understand what I'm saying.'

'Calm down, Rhea! Did something happen at work? Is your mom still pressuring you? Try to identify your problem, sweetheart. Relax, listen to some soothing music and think about what's bothering you. I may be able to come next week.'

'Can you? Please, Myra, that would be perfect. It's very depressing here. I have absolutely no one to talk to. Even the office environment is dreary. There's no pressure from Mumma about getting married. I feel like I'm at the end of my tether.'

Rhea could feel tears choking her. This was becoming a regular affair. She would cry at the drop of a hat.

'Don't work yourself up, babes. I can understand how difficult it must be. Relocating can be tough to deal with.'

Myra tried consoling her but Rhea's anxiety didn't ebb. Life was passing her by and she felt she was stuck in time. Moving to Hong Kong had not really given her the desired outcome. Each day after work, she came back to an impersonal, empty house. She suddenly remembered Happy's bedroom from long ago and was overcome with sadness. That memory was from another lifetime.

She cried for what she had lost along the way. She told herself that the tears were cathartic but the calm and relief that usually followed was missing.

Rhea went about her life in Hong Kong like a zombie. Nothing appealed to her anymore! She waited impatiently for Myra's arrival.

'What have you done to yourself? You seem to have lost at least 10 kilos! Is everything alright?' Myra was aghast on seeing the frail, waif-like girl who stood in front of her. 'What is bothering you so much, Riu? Is this only about the lack of company over here or is there something else? Is it about Rohit? Would it help if you spoke to him?'

'No! No! It's not about him. It's about me. I don't recognise the person I've turned into. I don't know what's wrong but nothing excites me anymore. This place is getting to me.'

'Maybe moving to Hong Kong wasn't such a good idea after all. You need to be around familiar faces. You've been through a lot of shit in life and maybe it was bottled up inside for all these years. It's a good thing that you're letting it out but you can't let it consume you to such an extent, sweetheart.'

'I know. I can't seem to help it.'

'Have you spoken to Aditi or Tapan lately?'

'I don't feel like talking to anyone.'

Myra had managed a week's leave from work, which now seemed less as she was worried about Rhea's state of mind.

'I am the black sheep of my family. Do you know both my sisters are married and have kids by now? Three of my younger cousins got married over the last one year. Am I destined to die an old maid? Nobody will say it to my face but everyone thinks I was too choosy and bull-headed and that's why I am where I am today—alone!'

'Don't wallow in self-pity. You are in a great position in life today. You're doing so well for yourself. When that special someone finally comes into your life, you'll laugh and wonder why you were being so silly! Pick yourself up and take some decisions. You're still young and life is beautiful; you just need to open your heart and mind to receive the good things that lie ahead. Remember, it's not over till the fat lady sings'

Just like that, Myra's words hit home! Rhea resolved to take charge of her life again.

Play!
The tide is high but I'm holding on
I'm gonna be your number one
I'm not the kind of girl who gives up just like that…

21

The Universe Replies

2013
Mumbai

Rhea was grateful to Myra for showing her the light. It was just what she needed and she consciously made an effort to do away with the pessimism.

She quit her job and moved back to Mumbai. Gurleen couldn't understand why she would leave a lucrative job at the peak of her career. Suddenly, Rhea's professional life was of some importance to her!

Rhea didn't have it in her to explain the reasons. Conversations with her mother became few and far between until she realised that this was the first time in her 33 years of existence that Gurleen hadn't wished her on her birthday.

Jaspal made some excuse on her behalf and he seemed almost apologetic about his wife's behaviour.

Rhea imagined her mother's trail of thought: 'What is so happy about her birthday? It's not like she's getting any younger. She's still unmarried; she doesn't even have a job anymore; she has no idea what she wants to do and she doesn't even want to come back to Jalandhar and stay with us. What is there to wish her for?'

While she couldn't help feeling bad about what her mother might have thought, she willfully erased these notions from her mind. Gurleen would come around some day, Rhea was sure of it.

Before the singledom crisis had hit, every guy Rhea knew used to be a friend or an acquaintance. Over the last few years, all the boys she met, even causally, had morphed into prospective grooms. She couldn't help the thought from entering her mind. Sometimes she wondered if she fell in love just to make sure that she still could.

She knew she had to consciously stop the emptiness from filling her heart and soul. She knew she didn't have to run after anyone or anything. She knew that when the time was right, the universe would make sure it fell in her lap.

All of 33, Rhea looked at her 15-year-old cousin playing video games on a computer and thought, 'Eighteen years ago, when I was his age, I was ready to get married!'

A shiver ran down her spine. Rhea was glad she had left that naïve girl far behind. She belonged to a bygone era.

What kind of life would she have led? Would she have had an identity of her own? She might have been a mother of teenage kids by now, maybe undergone a plastic surgery to enhance her nose or lips, like some rich, bored wives did!

As soon as that last thought came to her mind, she reprimanded herself. The world had taught her a thing or two and one of them was being non-judgmental.

Thinking about judgments, Rhea's mind wandered to how society and its people wouldn't wipe the 'broken engagement' and 'divorced' tag from her even though years had gone by. She might as well have tattooed it on her forehead. She gave a short laugh as she suddenly remembered Amitabh Bachchan's famous dialogue from *Deewaar*: '*Pehle uss aadmi ka sign le ke aao jisne mere haath par ye likh diya tha.*' On a lighter note, she wondered how she would look mouthing that dialogue.

Sometimes it was difficult to erase the feelings of embarrassment, self-loathing and regret that gnawed away on her insides. A year ago, Rhea had everything she could ever dream of: a loving boyfriend, a super job and a fantastic social circle!

Now, nothing!

But she was consciously making an effort to get her life back on track and be happy, above and beyond everything.

After coming back to Mumbai, Rhea involved herself in social service before she charted out her next course of action. However, after a few days of talking to representatives of an NGO, she didn't think social service was her calling.

She contemplated going to Igatpuri, in Nasik, to do a Vipassana course for 10 days. Maybe meditation was what she needed right now to cleanse the remaining negativity from her system.

Rhea needed to reconnect with herself. Somewhere along the road, a little girl had got lost and now she wanted to find her way back desperately.

Gurleen kept questioning her daughter's need to go for Vipassana. She'd read in a book: '*Most people do not listen with the intent to understand; they listen with the intent to reply.*' Her mother sometimes came across as that person.

'What is the need to do such things? These things are for old people and you're still young. Come back home.'

Rhea gave up trying to make her mother understand. She wouldn't go back to Jalandhar and face the inevitable inquisition from family and friends.

Her relationship with Rohit had left more than a bitter taste in her mouth. She was done chasing happiness and had no inclination left for anything that resembled a relationship or a romance.

After coming back from Hong Kong, Rhea had reconnected with Tapan. While talking to him one day, she mentioned that she was thinking of taking up Vipassana. Even though her mother refused to comprehend her, Rhea decided that she would go no matter what Gurleen said.

'Of course you should go if you really feel the need to. Now that you mention Vipassana, a friend of mine recently went to this place down south called Puratana. She totally loved the experience and was raving about the yoga and meditation centres there. You may also want to look it up as an option. The world is your oyster, lady! Go and seek whatever you desire.'

In the end, Tapan's recommendation appealed to Rhea more than going to Igatpuri. She made the booking, packed her bag and set off for Kerala.

According to Google, *'Puratana is a quaint township in Kerala's Kasaragod district. It is a town unmarred by modern-day means of communication and technology. Men and women from all over the world come here to find inner peace and tranquility to escape the daily rigmaroles of life. At Puratana, people believe in uniting humanity with the goal of having a peaceful existence in this world.'*

The mere idea of peace and tranquility was enough to lure Rhea. It was just the thing she needed. She made a reservation at the Aaryan Beach Guesthouse.

After checking in, she walked in the direction that the receptionist said her room was, soaking in all the sights and sounds around her.

Lost in the reverie, she suddenly bumped into someone and managed to topple all the contents of her handbag on the floor, as also the papers in his hands.

'I am sorry. I wasn't looki…'

She stopped dead in her tracks before she could finish her apology. No words came out after that. She just stared agape at him. It was as if her heart had found a new beat all of a sudden.

'Rhea! This has to be the sweetest coincidence ever.'

Only he could make her name sound musical.

'Liam!'

And then her vocabulary went dry. A huge smile slowly lit up his face.

His smile was worth more than a thousand words and it was the only thing Rhea remembered before she found herself in his arms.

Play!

Twenty-five years and I'm alive here still
Trying to get up that great big hill of hope
For a destination...

Acknowledgements

I have many people to thank, without whom the beginning of this fantastic literary journey would have been absolutely impossible.

I give my first thanks to the universe for making every little piece fall into place!

It was the silent yet rock solid support of my father, Arun Adesara, that made it possible for me to finally fulfill my long-standing dream of writing a book. My mother, Pragna, on the other hand, makes me want to be a better human being. Thank you, Ma, for being my strength and guiding light.

I cannot express in words the love I've got from my second set of parents—Shailesh and Dharini, my Mama and Mami. I was, am and will always be your eldest daughter. I'm deeply obliged and indebted to you both.

If not for the encouragement from my three aunts across the globe—Shital Gusani, Kashmira Jhaveri and Puja Soni—I would have found it difficult to move this story forward. They were among the first to read my absolutely raw first draft and sang my praises even then.

It takes a lot to drop everything and just write a book without knowing anything about the publishing world. You—Mahima Mehta—made me believe it was alright for me to do 'nothing else' but write this book, when most said otherwise. Thank you for helping me sail through that period of uncertainty.

My alter ego, Sonali Krishna. Babe, you rock! It was during our hour-long long-distance phone calls that I really understood

I wanted to get down to writing this book. Thank you. I will definitely 'pay it forward' in this lifetime.

Komal Sandhu, my stay with you in Bangalore while I was writing was a refreshing breather. Thank you for having me over and understanding that I really needed the time out!

Pallavi Khanna Sinha, you're a sweetheart! Thank you for making the effort to find out how I should go about getting published.

A big thank you to Paras Shah for making the time to read my first draft and pointing out some of my obvious mistakes.

Thank you, Amit Mukherjee, for playing the role of 'relationship coach'. You'll see that some of your beautiful words of advice to me have found their way into this story.

This book is in your hands today, thanks to the faith that Ajay Mago and Dipa Chaudhuri of Om Books International showed in my story. I thank you both for believing. My sincere thanks to my wonderful editor, Shreya Chakravertty, who is responsible for bringing this book out of its amateurish fold and making it shine with her little gems of advice. Thank you for helping me improve my work.

My family—Ashish, Reema, Killol, Nidhi, Niraj and Vaishali—you all make my world a happier place. Thank you for your love and support.

My soul sisters, Sheena Grewal and Divya Sahni, thank you for the unconditional love.

This section would be incomplete if I didn't mention the nurturing hands that have been instrumental in shaping me into the person I am today. I give my thanks to Sister Flavian, my principal; Mrs. Nargis Madon, Mrs. Kashmira Kotwal and Mrs. Gloria Prabal, my English teachers from Sacred Heart Convent School, Jamshedpur, and Sister Ananda from Sophia College, Mumbai. I am what I am because of you.

And last but not the least, thank you to my adorable baby—Tashi. I'm sorry I left you behind in Jamshedpur with the family during my writing pursuit. I know you understand. Woof!

A Very Special Thank You to: Khayyam Sahab, Majrooh Sultanpuri, Toni Braxton, Roxette, Gloria Gaynor, Coldplay, Queen, Bruce Springsteen, John Travolta, Jeff Conaway, Van Morrison, INXS, Pink Floyd, Atomic Kitten, Four Non Blondes, Javed Akhtar and Michael Jackson. Thank you for the music!